The Politics of Human Life

AF695111

This book centers on the notion of human life that lies at the foundation of contemporary thinking in the areas of ethics, law, and politics.

The book addresses the deep divide, characteristic of this thinking, between, on the one hand, those who wish to do away with any anthropological understandings of the human and appeal to mere facts delivered by science; and, on the other hand, critics who defend an anthropological understanding of human life that is tied to traditional, teleological, metaphysics. This opposition has, Piergiorgio Donatelli argues here, outlived its usefulness. Through a discussion of the intimate human spheres of reproduction, dying, and sexuality, he argues that we now live in a world characterized by new ways of living: novel rearrangements of emotions and the modification, and in some cases a radical rupture, in existing ideas of human life. These shifts challenge any established separation between facts and norms, between human life and its conceptualization. As such, it is argued here, they simultaneously offer the possibility of a new, socially articulated, understanding of the relationship between subjectivity and normativity.

Engaging pressing contemporary themes, this book will be invaluable to scholars in the fields of ethics, law, and political theory, and both analytic and continental philosophy.

Piergiorgio Donatelli is Professor of Philosophy and Head of the Department of Philosophy at Sapienza Università di Roma, Italy. He has written on the history of ethics, contemporary moral theory, bioethics, and on issues related to human life, as well as on J. S. Mill, Wittgenstein, Foucault, and Stanley Cavell.

The Politics of Human Life

Rethinking Subjectivity

Piergiorgio Donatelli

Routledge
Taylor & Francis Group
LONDON AND NEW YORK

First published 2021
by Routledge
2 Park Square, Milton Park, Abingdon, Oxon OX14 4RN

and by Routledge
605 Third Avenue, New York, NY 10158

Routledge is an imprint of the Taylor & Francis Group, an informa business

© 2021 Piergiorgio Donatelli

The right of Piergiorgio Donatelli to be identified as author of this work has been asserted by him in accordance with sections 77 and 78 of the Copyright, Designs and Patents Act 1988.

Translated by Sarin Marchetti
Originally published as *La vita umana in prima persona*, 2012, Laterza, Roma-Bari.

All rights reserved. No part of this book may be reprinted or reproduced or utilised in any form or by any electronic, mechanical, or other means, now known or hereafter invented, including photocopying and recording, or in any information storage or retrieval system, without permission in writing from the publishers.

Trademark notice: Product or corporate names may be trademarks or registered trademarks, and are used only for identification and explanation without intent to infringe.

British Library Cataloguing-in-Publication Data
A catalogue record for this book is available from the British Library

Library of Congress Cataloging-in-Publication Data
A catalog record has been requested for this book

ISBN: 978-1-138-04816-4 (hbk)
ISBN: 978-1-032-02088-4 (pbk)
ISBN: 978-1-315-17032-9 (ebk)

Typeset in Bembo
by Deanta Global Publishing Services, Chennai, India

Contents

Chapter 1

Reversing normative dispositives

1.1 Broadening the democratic imagination

In this book I defend freedom in such crucial areas of human life as reproduction, sexuality, and dying. Now, one might ask, why these moments in the first place? Because, I contend, these are the areas in which it has been traditionally claimed—that is, imposed through social practices and laws—that human life is *not* a place for the free expression of the self, but belongs, rather, to something else: to God, nature, the social order, or medical standards.

Is there anything remotely new to say about these themes? The situation we face looks as follows. On the one hand, there are countries, which are appallingly backward on these themes. On the other hand, it is not very interesting to stop short here, and remain stuck in one's country—or, better, in the most visible part of it. As will be clear later on, I claim that ethics has to do with the unbroken broadening of the space for discussion, which does not feed on closure toward alien experiences and judgments. Confrontation is always over concrete issues: it has nothing to do with abstract flights of thought, but rather revolves around the experiences of those—individuals, groups, communities, nations—whose very imagination broadened with regard to matters of opinion, conduct, and what we can do as subjects with moral aspirations. Moral thought should not fall prey to the experience of those caught in their dull beliefs and conducts, unwilling to speak to, and learn from, others: those who, hypocritically and lacking any reflective capacity, walk a path in which the things done do not chime with the things lived. A life of this kind is indeed limited and dull, and hence morally reproachable.

We should broaden the democratic imagination and take into consideration both the associated life of those various countries which genuinely took in the transformations of our ways of living and the theoretical reflection and intellectual discussion which backed them up. Only then could we ask what we might say and want in connection with values and conducts. But, once again, is there really anything new to say? Hasn't everything already been secured both theoretically and concretely, so that we should simply move on and pursue other goals? In a way, we should answer in the affirmative. It is a mature society that rules those areas of human existence where crucial interests and projects nestle: giving birth to babies autonomously and responsibly by employing diagnostic and reproductive technologies; choosing the ways in which we shall die with reference to the ample spectrum of instruments and technologies involving the intervention of medical staff, and our choices to use such technologies or refusing to; living our sexual and intimate life in accordance with our ways of being, dethroning the antiquated model of heterosexual marriage; raising kids in many sorts of ways, as a couple or single. It is the mark of a mature society that such areas are regulated with reference to laws and acquired social practices which take the interests of the individuals in and guarantee the respect of their freedom—as we expect any decent society worth the name would consider as acquired the equality of its citizens whatever their sex, the color of the skin, or job. It is certainly the mark of a serious and solid society that questions such as these—related to matters of knowledge and value alike—become part of our shared heritage. This was, for example, John Stuart Mill's view. We try out and experiment with opinions, theories, rules of conduct, institutions, and, at a certain point, we reach the conviction that a certain belief or way of organizing society is grounded because it has been exposed to every possible criticism and comparison with reality. To question one's convictions and ways of organizing society does not mean to challenge the very grounds of our moral conduct: quite the contrary, says Mill, it is the only way to prove them grounded.[1]

The progress of our societies in the areas of human life I have mentioned has been, historically speaking, rather irregular, and the technological transformations that contributed to the modification of the beginning and end of life by means of techniques of assisted reproduction and life-support machines is quite a recent event; but we have now gathered sufficient evidence and experimentations showing how it is only by respecting individual freedom and promoting the interests of those involved that we actually guarantee moral attention and concern. Suicide, sexuality, and reproduction follow rather uneven paths: the topic of rational suicide is as old as the Western philosophical tradition, with its supporters—from Seneca to Montaigne to Hume—and detractors—from Plato to Aquinas to Kant—; sexuality has been treated in the most diverse and discontinuous ways, despite the long centuries of

Christian hegemony. The topic of reproductive freedom is, on the other hand, a quite recent one, and went hand in hand with the issue of the emancipation of women—it originated in the Italian Renaissance and bloomed in the eighteenth and nineteenth centuries. However, these various advances have been secured once the forms of life at the heart of democratic societies took center stage. Can we truly think that now, in our democratic societies, these areas of life should be regulated—through the law and social practices—unlike other areas of our existence? Why should our societies regulate work, political representation, or freedom of expression differently from reproduction, sexual relationships, or death? Once the democratic framework is secured, it does not seem to be reasonable at all to think that there are areas of life falling outside of it.

This is, once again, an argument put forward by Mill, offered in defense of a radical reformation of the social institution of marriage itself.[2] Mill asks, in fact, how is at all possible for us to regulate society according to principles of justice and prudence, and at the very same time treat the family differently—the family being such a crucial site for the education of the sentiments and opinions of those who will (the offspring) and already do (parents) take care of society in view of these very same democratic principles. How is it possible to justify the asymmetry between the family and the rest of society, then? This line of reasoning by Mill is also still very much relevant regarding the new themes of human life discussed in this book. But now, unlike Mill, we have a rich and articulated history behind us: one's imagination can be broadened not only by looking to the present, thanks to the global conversation we may now enjoy, but also by looking back to history and considering the acquisitions of our societies which became part of them. From this point of view, the extension of freedom and the consideration of the interests to these areas of life—reproduction, sexuality, and death—looks nowadays as rather obvious and indisputable.

1.2 Ethics and the broad bases of experience

What I have been elaborating so far is a line of reasoning by which we should take the social practices and the regulations pertaining to the areas of human life I have mentioned as a datum no longer under dispute. The thesis of this book, however, is that this is hardly enough. This argument from past acquisitions is not enough for several reasons. Here I would like to list two: I shall introduce the first in this paragraph and the second in the following one.

The first reason has to do with the very nature of ethics, broadly understood as what gets sedimented in attitudes and various forms of approval and disapproval such as sentiments and language, but also practices and rules, which can also be codified and find expression in the law. In the perspective I shall outline—in which ethics is understood as the expression of forms of life, processes of civilization, and waves of human reactions cementing the many kinds of relationships we entertain with each other—every acquisition that consolidates in whatever shape—in laws or the widespread reception of a certain belief (e.g., the platitude according to which it is wicked and stupid to discriminate against people on the basis of alleged racial considerations)—gets its strength from this underlying basis without there being any further, independent ones. That moral beliefs get solidity from an independent basis is a widespread assumption in philosophical circles, which has been advanced by a number of different approaches: for example, by those claiming for the existence of eternal truths, to be found in the nature of things, which reason is capable of seizing—exemplified, in the metaphysical tradition, e.g. by the Thomists—; or by those who think that reason, even if it does not discover anything deep about the world, still endows us with the capacity to make us conscious of the duties which characterize us a priori as rational beings—as with the Kantian tradition. Alternatively, if we think that this solidity cannot be secured in these ways, that it cannot be so easily severed from the vast mass of contingencies constituting our lives, then we simply cannot disconnect what rightly appears as grounded and unassailable from the mobile mass of attitudes, human relations, and activities underlying it. What seems to be unassailable is simply what we strongly care about: the basis of its solidity is also the basis of our attitudes and of our world.

The idea by which, in order to make sense of moral beliefs, institutions, and all that which has solidified in structures apparently purified from the mass of human attitudes and activities, we need to start from the bottom, that is, from the mass of human responses and relations, has been explored along different avenues. Amartya Sen has provided an acute account of a tradition that made this idea central to its self-image, which he calls anti-transcendental, and which he traces back to the Scottish philosophical line and its protagonists David Hume and Adam Smith.[3] Mill was equally part of this line, even if he integrated it with a different one, to which I shall come back later. I myself, in this book, will put forward arguments and ideas in the wake of both Mill's original elaboration of this anti-transcendental line and a completely independent twentieth-century tradition that draws on Wittgenstein's philosophy and equally develops the idea that, in ethics, we should move from the bottom.[4]

According to this perspective, then, those beliefs and institutions we cherish the most and that we depict as unassailable are, exactly, *what we cherish the most*, that is, are to be traced back to the core of attitudes and the whirl of human activities and responses in which these beliefs and institutions play a role. This point has been clearly stated by Mill.[5] He held two theses apparently in tension with one another, but which we can hold together once we endorse the explanation of what makes a belief solid and grounded offered by the anti-transcendentalist line. Mill held, on the one hand, that those beliefs which underwent criticism and successfully faced the challenge of experience earn our respect, become solid, and give us all the reasons to consider them as true. An advanced and progressive society is grounded on a growing core of beliefs of just this kind, which makes less and less sense to challenge. This is the thesis that claims both the actuality and the positive value of the accumulation of knowledge and convictions in every field, scientific and practical alike. We experiment, for example, with our own conceptions about the nature of the physical world, but we also experiment with our own conception of what a good organization of political representation might look like: civilized societies put together a notable supply of these kinds of convictions which have proved the test of experience. But Mill adds a further, rather different thesis. He, in fact, claims, on the other hand, that every time we treat a belief or a rule of conduct as something acquired, as something taken for granted, those beliefs and rules begin to lose touch with their underlying expressive core: with the reasoning, experimentations, and encounters with experience they underwent, which bestow solidity on them and strengthened them. As Mill writes, a belief is not grounded because we consider it to be above all criticisms and proofs, but rather it is grounded because it keeps winning the challenge of such trials. If we understand these beliefs as simply acquired and assimilated, we actually reverse the very order of explanation and picture them as grounded on foundations of their very own in no need of further proof, of further challenges from reality.

Here we find the sketch of a clear line of thinking which exhorts us to perform two tasks at once: to appreciate our very capacity to cherish and put to use grounded beliefs and rules of conduct, which is a distinctive feature of our processes of civilization, and at the same time not to stop the activity of questioning them and proving them against ever new experiences. This is the first line of thinking that I will be employing in my treatment of the themes revolving around human life as discussed in this book. Democratic and liberal acquisitions on these themes are indeed precious and hardly negotiable, and yet they are such exactly because we do not put them away and shield them from the encounter with new experiences. The value and ground of these acquisitions, which look like platitudes to us, would be corrupted and turn into an empty shell only if they were not continuously nurtured by the encounter with experience, and hence with critical thinking and questioning—and this is exactly what happens to dogmas, writes Mill, when left playing the role of sentinels as against the possibility, for experience, to breathe fresh air into the minds holding them.[6] If a belief is taken to be simply acquired, it means that we have started to cut the thread which connects it to the world of attitudes and activities which make it alive and active in the first place.

1.3 Modernity and tradition

An independent line of reasoning equally spurs us not to be satisfied with considering the beliefs and regulations over the topics concerning human life as simply acquired. As we have seen, what appears to be simply acquired needs to be seen in a different light: this task is an essential part of the need to breathe new life into acquired truth, which Mill talks about. But now I would like to introduce and discuss a particular idea about the topics covered in the book. By putting to work one's imaginative resources—which exceed the narrow boundaries of any particular place—we have secured the liberties and concerns pertaining to birth, sexuality, and dying as an integral part of our democratic life. Yet, the way in which we have acquired them has contributed to hiding the bases which made these acquisitions possible in the first place and still keep them alive, that is, the ample areas of experience that made these acquisitions important and no longer negotiable. There is an influential picture of what it has meant to acquire these liberties and concerns in said, pivotal areas of human life—a picture which hides the very bases of such achievements. This is the very picture I would like to criticize in this book. According to the dominant picture, the consequence of the acquisition of freedom for women in reproductive choices, the freedom of the dying person to end her life voluntarily, and the freedom to build a sexual life expressive of one's subjective and creative conception of relationships, bodies, and pleasures, is the subtraction of these areas of life from an entire world of perceptions, meanings, attitudes, and relationships, freeing them from all this and bringing them under the pool of light represented by the modern and civil principles of the respect of freedom and the consideration of the interests involved.

The clash at the heart of modernity, which resulted in the legitimation and spreading of liberal acquisitions on the themes of human life, has been since portrayed as follows. On the one hand, there are the advocates of the traditional world, which has been taken for granted once and for all, who talk about objective places—such as that of human nature—by employing the distinctive instruments of the pre-modern worldview, which we can summarize, following Alasdair MacIntyre's lead, along three axes: a teleological conception of nature; a hierarchical and metaphysical understanding of the social order; and a heteronomous theological view.[7] As a consequence, the various areas of human life—for example, the three I shall discuss in the book: reproduction, sexuality, and death—have been variously considered as the expression of the intrinsic ends of nature; as part of a social space organized according to metaphysical distinctions and rankings (e.g., between men and women, clergy and secular people, etc.); and as regulated according to duties derived from the law of God. On the other hand, there are those who struggled to make this world and views look obsolete, celebrating the space of human freedom and interests freed from these constraints. In this light, the advocates of the objective space of women's modesty, of intrinsic teleology as a sign of a divine plan inscribed in the pregnant body and fetus, of the teleology and intrinsic order belonging to our very sexual nature (we are either males or females), of the teleology of life making its course and fully in the hands of God for as long as it is in his plans to make it last: they all had to face those who challenged the alleged intrinsic quality and objective character of these circumstances of human life in order to defend human freedom and interests, thus putting aside what these circumstances have meant to the subjects involved, and questioning the duties and attitudes which have been associated with them for centuries. This is the dominant image of the clash which saw the supporters of freedom victorious, and from whose victories we have inherited the recent acquisitions in these issues. In contemporary terms, we have, for example, the freedom and responsibility of women over their sexual and reproductive choices, interests to be taken care of—theirs and the prospective ones of the unborn baby—while there is nothing like modesty or the sacred character of pregnancy to honor.

The philosophical picture just described, which I shall be criticizing, is a rather influential one, but it has a non-philosophical counterpart which is prominent in the cultural debate on these themes. The latter often takes the following form. The successful struggle against the traditional conceptions was able to get rid of that stock of values, but it did not replace them with others, leaving the field open to egoisms and to a disarticulation of the human fabric, so to speak. Freedom and the promotion of interests that inspired the various democratic acquisitions are depicted as thin principles freed from the thicker soil in which human life grew and thrived. This is, for one thing, the standard criticism advanced from the conservative side to the empty and pernicious character of the principles of freedom and the quality of life. But this is a line equally promoted by a portion of the critics of conservatism. According to one of its versions, egoisms and the apparent lack of authentic moral concerns featuring human conduct are but the effect of the liberation from ancient ties prompted by the many circumstances related to the revolution of mores in the 1960s and 70s. An emblematic exponent of this critical line was Pier Paolo Pasolini. As he wrote, the "the power of consumption… took hold of the exigencies of freedom – liberal and progressist alike, so to speak –, and, in so doing, it jeopardized them and changed their nature."[8] Pasolini can be read as someone who considered the contemporary forms of freedom as incapable of giving voice to an authentic anthropology, to a set of values, or rather as someone who would actually desire that our forms of freedom could give body to an anthropology, but who acknowledges nonetheless its failure, acknowledging the "ruins of values" in which we currently find ourselves.[9] At any rate, according to Pasolini, we would have gained freedom at the price of having given away the wider anthropological soil and the values it nourished.

These considerations are grounded in the picture I would like to criticize: they depict the victory of the principles of freedom and the promotion of interests as the liberation from the space of perceptions and attitudes surrounding the crucial areas of human life such as reproduction, sexuality, and death. But, if we picture modern principles in this way, we hide the wider empirical bases which make them alive, the vast areas of experience which make these acquisitions important and vital to us. We do not see how these acquisitions did not in fact brush away the traditional anthropological soil, leaving room for liberal principles to operate, but rather how they have transformed human relations, perceptions, and attitudes by re-articulating them: they did not simply get rid of them. We should be able to appreciate these transformations and what they have given life to, to appreciate the modern and democratic acquisition from the point of view of the low, of the web of experiences and human life in which they are rooted.

The young Mill, in the 1830s, had this problem in clear view and claimed how a liberal project should not be thought of as aimed at weakening one's beliefs and eroding their only bases, but rather as a positive program which would transform beliefs and plant new ones. Mill reads an utterly negative and destructive tendency in skeptical Enlightenment and portions of Jeremy Bentham's work as well. Their goal was that of undermining the felt respect for past doctrines and institutions: they "can perceive what is false, but not what is true; [they] awaken the human mind to the inconsistencies and absurdities of time-sanctioned opinions and institutions, but substitute nothing in the place of what they take away."[10] However, they fulfilled a crucial and most pressing role once we situate their interventions in their historical context, and read these philosophical and cultural traditions as a reaction to a cultural and social condition in which "mankind have outgrown old institutions and old doctrines, and have not yet acquired new ones."[11] In the essay on "Bentham," Mill writes:

> An age of formalism in the Church and corruption in the State, when the most valuable part of the meaning of traditional doctrines had faded from the minds even of those who retained from habit a mechanical belief in them, was the time to raise up all kinds of sceptical philosophy.[12]

The skeptical philosophers lived at a time in which the very meaning of believing in a truth had been shaken, a time characterized by a hardly reconcilable gap between the doctrines which express and regulate the life of people and this life itself, a time marked by a lack of conviction, by a condition of disillusion toward the possibility of having any trust in things at all. In Mill's perspective, their error was that of "mistaking the state of things with which they had always been familiar, for the universal and natural condition of mankind."[13] The skeptical condition is not that in which a certain truth is believed and endorsed, but rather that in which it is no more possible to believe in it, in which the intellectual horizon itself that made it possible to believe in a cluster of truths crumbled under our feet, but in which it is also possible to get a glimpse of the formation of further horizons which make it possible to believe in other things. This is why he wrote that "to have erroneous convictions is one evil; but to have no strong or deep-rooted convictions at all, is an enormous one."[14] According to Mill, we should not take the skeptical side of reform movements as the only side; the other side is that in which new beliefs and social forms are cemented by earning our respect and conviction. In the struggle against the traditional worldview, the skeptical reformers have committed to the dismantlement of an entire territory, but in so doing, they captured one side of the story only; the other one being that in which alternative territories are explored, with new ways of living which allow us to embrace new beliefs.

In this book, I seek to explore this idea by Mill. The acquisitions in those areas of human life such as reproduction, death, and sexuality went together with a picture in which deep perceptions and convictions (about the body in the first place) have been cast away in the belief that what we are left with is an empty space protected by principles that are but the expression of such notions as autonomy and the promotion of interests. But this is *not* the case. These acquisitions have a skeptical side to them—consisting in the taking apart of conceptions and attitudes—but they also have a different side, in which the terrain that those conceptions and attitudes insisted on has been transformed: a transformative and constructive side that cannot be fully accounted for in terms of universal principles, but which should be brought back to their bases, to the lower floors of the edifice of moral thought, made of the frameworks which articulate the density of human life, of what reproduction, sexuality, and death mean to us.

Here we find a second reason that prompts us to go back to the democratic achievements in these areas and to consider them as not simply (or fully, as yet) acquired. They demand to be rethought since we have formed a picture that needs to be revised, a skeptical picture that hides what we have achieved from us. It hides from us both what the liberals care about and what the conservatives champion. We then need to rethink this clash. To this task Chapter 2 will be dedicated.

Notes

1 John Stuart Mill, *On Liberty*, in *Collected Works of John Stuart Mill*, Vol. XVIII: *Essays on Politics and Society*, ed. by J.M. Robson, Toronto: University of Toronto Press, 1977, Chapters 2 and 3. For my interpretation, see Piergiorgio Donatelli, *Introduzione a Mill*, Roma-Bari: Laterza, 2007.

2 John Stuart Mill, *The Subjection of Women*, in *Collected Works of John Stuart Mill*, Vol. XXI: *Essays on Equality, Law, and Education*, ed. by J.M. Robson, Toronto: University of Toronto Press, 1984.

3 Amartya Sen, *The Idea of Justice*, London: Penguin Books, 2009. An examination of this Scottish line has been offered by Eugenio Lecaldano, *Hume e la nascita dell'etica contemporanea*, Roma-Bari: Laterza, 1991.

4 I address this tradition—which has as its crucial authors Iris Murdoch, Stanley Cavell, and Cora Diamond—in Piergiorgio Donatelli, *Manières d'être humain. Une autre philosophie morale*, Paris: Vrin, 2015.

5 John Stuart Mill, *On Liberty*, op. cit., Chapter 2.

6 John Stuart Mill, *ibid.*, p. 248. In cases such as these, Mill writes, "an hereditary creed…to be received passively, not actively…remains as it were outside the mind, incrusting and petrifying it against all other influences addressed to the higher parts of our nature: manifesting its power by not suffering any fresh and living conviction to get in, but itself doing nothing for the mind or heart except standing sentinel over them to keep them vacant."

7 Alasdair MacIntyre, *After Virtue. A Study in Moral Theory* (1981), Notre Dame: University of Notre Dame Press, 1984.
8 Pier Paolo Pasolini, "Il coito, l'aborto, la falsa tolleranza del potere, il conformismo dei progressisti," in *Scritti corsari* (1975), Milano: Garzanti, 1990, p. 99. See also the other essays in the volume—in particular, those on abortion.
9 Pier Paolo Pasolini, "Pannella and Dissent," in *Lutheran Letters*, New York: Carcanet Press, 1987, p. 56. See also "My 'Accattone' on TV after the Genocide," *ibid.*, pp. 100–104: at p. 101 we read that "Between 1961 and 1975 something essential changed: a genocide took place. A whole population was culturally destroyed." These punctual references to Pasolini do not do justice to an author who would be very instructive to examine in depth for the perspective advanced in this book.
10 John Stuart Mill, "Bentham," in *Collected Works of John Stuart Mill,* Vol. X, *Essays on Ethics, Religion and Society*, ed. by J.M. Robson, Toronto: University of Toronto Press, 1969, p. 79.
11 John Stuart Mill, "The Spirit of the Age" (1831), in *Collected Works of John Stuart Mill*, Vol. XXII, *Newspapers Writings,* Part I, ed. by A.P. Robson and J.M. Robson, Toronto: University of Toronto Press, 1986, p. 230.
12 John Stuart Mill, "Bentham," op. cit., p. 80.
13 John Stuart Mill, "Coleridge," in *Collected Works of John Stuart Mill,* Vol. X, *Essays on Ethics, Religion and Society*, ed. by J.M. Robson, Toronto: University of Toronto Press, 1969, p. 132.
14 John Stuart Mill, "The Spirit of the Age," op. cit., p. 233.

Chapter 2

Liberals and conservatives

Rethinking the clash

2.1 Reactions

I have been claiming that acquired beliefs, social practices, and institutions in the crucial areas of human life need to be rethought and revisited. This is because, as Mill claimed, each acquired belief and rule tends to lose touch with the living bases that made us subscribe to it in the first place. As a consequence, in the moments taken as paradigmatic, it might seem that reproductive freedom, the freedom to choose when to die, and the freedom to give personal expression to one's sexuality simply derive from the application of the principle of freedom to these areas, being a straightforward effect of this principle. In this way, the meaning of these liberties is only related to the universal principle of freedom and loses touch with the much broader and more articulated bundle of meanings intertwined with what it means to claim such liberties: for example, the meaning of one's body as a woman, to think of it as a female body and its reproductive capacity as part of one's subjectivity, as a part of one's open field of choices, and as a domain of life in which it makes sense to choose.

I have also claimed that the particular unfolding of these acquisitions needs to be thought anew. This story witnessed the clash between the advocates of objective areas—teleological, social, and theological alike—in which to place the various spheres of human life, and the defenders of the individual as a free agent with interests of her own. The character of this clash has facilitated a particular representation of the terms debated. The defenders of modernity pictured themselves as engaged in the dismissing of objective spaces in order to claim the content of those areas as something completely other from such objective spaces: namely, freedom and interests, which are something that can be claimed by anyone at any time, as they neither subscribe to any teleological conceptions of nature and hierarchical conceptions of the social order nor make reference to the divine law. On the other hand, the advocates of the older world saw themselves as engaged in the defense of conceptions of human nature, society, and God jeopardized by the new ideas. For this reason, the clash has the skeptical feature indicated by Mill. It might seem that the vindication of freedom and interests was a purely negative task, aimed at the destruction of any horizon that would make room for strong and deep-seated opinions since the battle was against what at the time was perceived as the only horizon available—the one horizon I have characterized with reference to the combination of a teleological conception of nature, a hierarchical conception of the social order, and a theological understanding of reality. It is for this reason that the reformers and the skeptical thinkers of the Enlightenment alike (in Mill's sense) were engaged in the debunking of any conception that would speak of an intrinsic feature of nature and the social order, and in the abolition of any reference to God, since in such conditions, the appeal to an objective dimension in which to place human action would deprive them of the very possibility and space to claim human freedom and interests.

For example, the objective dimension that generates the entire cluster of perceptions, attitudes, language, and hence duties expressed in the concept of women's modesty is simply unfit for women to be able to claim their individual and subjective freedom and interests. In this light, Hume's strategy was that of relocating modesty and chastity in the domain of the artificial virtues, that is, among those convictions useful for, or rather harmful to, society, depending on the time and situation, debunking, in so doing, the objective dimension of modesty. This shift parallels his debunking of the objective dimension that makes dying an area in which it is impossible to have interests and exercise one's freedom and in light of which suicide is simply unthinkable.[1] The appeal to customs and conventions is, as a matter of fact, a step which, from Montaigne on, has been taken to show how there is nothing objective and intrinsic in how nature appears to us, no intrinsic special order, with no God as the source of objective duties and orders. An author such as Sade, for example, in his novels —at times in amusing ways while at others in sickening ones—variously experiments with what it would mean to take what is usually shown to belong to the constitutive nature of humanity as merely conventional, as something which we can easily consider as absent or differently arranged. A very enjoyable novel such as *Aline and Valcour* explores these various possibilities, questioning all those pillars of civil coexistence in the form of received and reinforced prohibitions, such as murder, sexual practices that do not conform to Christian conjugal duties, divorce, anthropophagy, atheism, blasphemy, and suicide.[2]

On the other hand, and conversely so, the advocates of the older world defended what, in their eyes, also appeared as the only horizon that allowed for ingrained beliefs and hence duties and an genuine moral life. From their point of view, to deny and repudiate objective spaces for human action to nestle in—such as those represented by a teleological conception of nature, a hierarchic conception of the social order, and an understanding of God as a source of duty—would have meant renouncing the very possibility of articulating a background against which to account for actions as something capable of being understood with reference to the fabric of human and moral descriptions. From their point of view, for example, criticism of the objective space of women's modesty amounted to criticism of the moral space of sexuality as such. Sade is once again very instructive on this point. On the one hand, as I have suggested, he experimented with the idea that there are no objective spaces and that it is possible to open different conventional spaces in view of building alternative moral conceptions and practices. On the other hand, he took a rather different path from the one I have been suggesting, showing that the consequence of giving up the traditional, objective space—that is, the theological-Christian one—would be the disappearance of moral laws as a whole, hence the liceity of murder and cruelty in its most diverse forms he describes. In subscribing to this second line, Sade partakes in the influential tradition of thought to which, in the following century, Dostoevsky gives voice through the words of Ivan Karamazov as reported by Smerdyakov: "if there's no infinite God, then there's no virtue either, and no need of it at all."[3] Once the Christian objective framework has fallen, anything goes and the very capacity to make moral distinctions is lost.

These are nothing but reactions, Mill argues.[4] The defenders of freedom and interests, in their opposition to the traditional framework, have the impression of struggling against any objective dimension possible, and that morality can be reconstructed only somewhere else, in a space devoid of conceptions of human nature, society, and, of course, God, in the free space in which freedom is at work and in which individual interests lie. Now, it is quite hard to recap and digest the thought of a classic author such as Hume in a few sentences, but we might say that an aspect of his work can be read as the inauguration of a tradition which dispenses with the notion of an alleged objective space, of overall frameworks—natural, social, and theological alike—, and offers an account of morality on alternative grounds. That said, Bentham will read Hume as someone still very much dear to a notion of human nature that prevented him from fully emancipating interests and hence spaces of freedom from external objective notions.[5] The advocates of past ideas, on the other hand, work under the impression that the framework of human activities held together by a teleological conception of nature and a hierarchical notion of society ruled by the divine law—which grew during the centuries of the Christian Middle Ages—is the only space capable of hosting moral life, reading in this clash a blow to morality. As a consequence, the conservatives think that once the framework of the social order—that is, of tradition—, nature, and God is jeopardized, what we are left with is the impossibility of articulating the moral life. However, if we read these two lines of the answer as reactions, we could reinterpret the clash from the ground up: the defenders of freedom and interests are struggling to transform inherited objective spaces into alternative spaces, while conservatives are struggling to preserve not so much *the* only possible form of objective space but rather *a* certain space, a distinctive conception of a background that allows for the expression of the values dear to them.

We can witness the continuation of this clash up to the present stage. This is the thesis I would like to articulate and defend. I am in fact convinced that we can still detect a contemporary version of the clash, where the shape is that of a reaction—that is, similar to how Mill depicted the clash in the first decades of the nineteenth century. Conservatives defend objective spaces—in particular, that of human nature and corollary notions—as the only way to defend morality as a whole. Liberals, on the other hand, reject all kinds of objective space, and in particular the relevance of the reference to human nature and corollary notions. Read as a form of reaction, the clash opens up to a different interpretation: we may offer a representation of it which helps to transform our self-understanding and the understanding of the acquisitions and disagreements animating our societies. In this light, the clash would turn out to be between defenders of different objective spaces, between different conceptions of human life: between conceptions of what it means to reproduce, die, and have a sexual life. But in order to be so understood, the clash needs to recruit broader bases of attitudes, human responses, perceptions, and concepts, so as not to make it look like a clash between defenders of universal and thin concepts—such as those of freedom and interests—and the advocates of thick frameworks—such as that of human nature.

2.2 Utilitarianism

A characteristic way in which this clash has reached us is in the form of the contrast between liberals and conservatives. In my use of the two terms, the liberals defend ever new spaces of freedom and human interests to be taken into consideration and promoted as a way of breaking free of those intrinsic, objective, conceptions defended by the conservatives. In terms of contemporary philosophical theory, liberals assume two characteristic shapes: namely, utilitarianism and Kantian contractualism. Utilitarianism and Kantianism offer clear accounts and defenses of two important and almost inescapable sources of moral concern: the former thematizes the centrality of the consequences of our deeds, the relationship between our actions and the empirical, worldly, conditions that such actions contribute to bringing about (happiness, unhappiness, quality of life); the latter thematizes the morality featuring in our actions when directed toward other rational agents and affecting them accordingly, highlighting the conditions they impose on our choices for the kinds of action they are, the limit brought by the performance of a line of conduct which we would describe as, say, theft, lying, or murder on our will. Now, we can comment on, and put forward a number of criticisms of, how these two philosophical theories account for these sources of moral concern.

Utilitarianism gives voice to the idea that, in the ethical domain, what we do has a certain weight because it takes into consideration the well-being of our fellow human beings—or of an even broader range of beings that includes all sentient beings, in their capacity to feel pleasure or pain, to express preferences and interests. The recommended conduct—that is, what it is right to do—is that which would likely produce the greatest amount of value in terms of pleasure or satisfied preferences—the principle of maximization. Contemporary utilitarianism is a clear expression of the perspective I am attributing to the liberals. This is particularly clear in bioethical reflection, in which utilitarianism has proved to be a most fertile theoretical approach. In the bioethical domain, utilitarianism aimed at unmasking a condition in which, as Mill wrote, "the most valuable part of the meaning of traditional doctrines had faded from the minds even of those who retained from habit a mechanical belief in them,"[6] and criticized those duties and conceptions of human nature unable to reach and account for experience. Peter Singer is an emblematic author in this respect. As he writes, old traditional ethics—that of the Biblical Decalogue, which invested birth and death with a sacral aura made of absolute duties—is inadequate to account for the moral dilemmas we face.[7] An ethics of this kind is unable to take into account the moral relevance of the life of other (non-human) beings on the planet. It is unable to make sense of the dilemmas at the beginning of life, where the imperative to reproduce in circumstances when we predict a miserable existence, or in light of demographical or environmental considerations, is ungrounded. Such a perspective is equally blind to the problems at the end of life, where the imperative never to kill innocent individuals completely misses the issues involved in those situations in which people in great misery and without any perspective of recovery ask to die.

As a consequence, we can see here at work the skeptical side expected of a philosophy which, free of prejudices, investigates the nature of our moral conceptions of human life and the duties associated with it, and verifies that such conceptions and duties are unable to express our moral concerns, or not any longer, at least. Utilitarianism, and in particular an author such as Singer, has helped us to dismantle a situation in which the old doctrines were unable to reach and articulate the experience of the subjects involved. The criticisms advanced by utilitarianism to the traditions of vitalism and natural law—as well as to the massive machinery of deontology—made it possible to appreciate the current scene. For example, in matters of end-of-life choices, this approach made it possible to acknowledge how the appeal to the absolute prohibition to kill is actually unhelpful to account for the new medical circumstances characterized by a transformation of the very concepts of medical care and treatment. In such circumstances, the proper goals of medicine can no longer be taken for granted, and, as a consequence, once these goals have been unsettled, it is not possible to take for granted that these goals truly are good for everybody—as is the case for all those that Plato called the arts, in which the goal is taken for granted—say, in architecture, where the goal is to build structures that last. Once the framework of medical science is unsettled, what gains greater prominence is not the received goal of the medical art, but rather the individual ones of the patient. As a consequence, in this renewed context, the very role of the medical practitioner needs to be radically rethought: we need to rethink medical practice and duties in light of these changes. Similarly, the conception of life as a process endowed with a teleology of its very own—a teleology that we should simply honor, and in which we cannot intervene—is emptied to the extent that life-functions have been replaced, and hence it is no longer possible to clearly distinguish what is natural from what is artificial, for example, in circumstances characterized by natural processes (the life of an organism) on which we intervene pervasively. This teleological conception, with its distinctive and complex machinery of absolute duties and prohibitions, is clearly a survival, in the medical context, of the background which, as we have seen, started to crumble with modernity. However, it is the technological interventions on human life that have contributed to definitely undermining its bases: one of the fundamental roles played by utilitarianism, then, has been that of showing the emptiness of the teleological framework and mindset.

Utilitarianism played a skeptical role, and yet it did not settle for that: it also offered a general account of moral life. Utilitarianism didn't just wish to criticize a number of absolute prohibitions, such as the prohibition to kill innocents, within the medical practice; its aim was not only to dismantle the sacred (and hence untouchable) character of certain aspects of life; nor to simply criticize the stupidity that made us put human interests at the center to the detriment of the much broader ones of the animal kingdom. Its aims were not only skeptical with reference to such ways of understanding life and morality. An author such as Singer draws a general conclusion from the skeptical side of utilitarianism: namely, that it is precisely human actions as such that lack any moral weight. The human circumstances as described from our individual point of view have no moral weight whatsoever: the whole weight is brought back to the force of the normative dispositive of the maximization of interests. The way in which we should be struck and moved by the duty to help someone in great pain who asks us to die; in which it seems serious yet reasonable to interrupt a pregnancy; in which it seems horrible to consider primates as entertainment in circuses or, even worse, laboratory animals for experimentation, or as hunting prey: what strikes and hurts us from a moral point of view in these examples would have nothing to do with what we read in our actions or in the circumstances in which we are involved. There is nothing to what it is and means, for us, pregnancy or reproduction, to approach death, or the relationship with beings so close to us and yet so distant from us such as chimpanzees and orangutans: there is nothing to all this—in our reactions, perceptions, and ways to describe these circumstances—that is capable of determining what we *should be doing*. All that we should be doing is to be understood in terms of the production of the state of things that include, for example, satisfied preferences—a production understood as a relation between two or more events that do not concern us in any special way as a certain kind of human agent. All that could help us in understanding what those interests that move our moral response amount to in such contexts should be done without. If we read Singer, this side of the criticism I am mounting against him—and which Cora Diamond mounted with regard to animal ethics[8]—could fail to make it to the surface. We are indeed shocked by reading about the torture inflicted on animals or by the contradictions inbuilt into the traditional, Christian, defense of the prohibition to kill innocent human beings, and yet what shocks us and moves us is not part of what makes these conceptions morally wrong: it is rather part of the assorted human reactions from which we should emancipate ourselves in order to reason clearly over the value involved in these situations and the causal relations that relate this value to the various sources of the foreseen consequences, among which there are human beings acknowledging such consequences and acting on this knowledge.

Here we see the two aspects that I have indicated in Chapter 1: on the one hand, the distinction between normative dispositives and the broader bases of human responses; on the other, the distinction between universal principles and frameworks. Singer rules out the possibility that the broader bases of our moral approval might play a role. On the other hand, he rules out there being anything significant to register in what the natural framework means for us; in what pregnancy, birth, and dying mean for us; in what it means for us to face individuals who look at us, touch us, and communicate with us, and yet who are not human like us. All that is morally salient, for Singer, is captured by the notion of interest. The rest—for example, the diverse ways in which giving birth and dying have a weight and create a rich texture in our lives, the background against which the single issues eventually stand out, such as how to consider newborns and persons in a persistent vegetative state—simply disappears. From these notable exclusions some precise normative consequences follow, which are an integral part of Singer's moral system of challenging all the so-called taboos—in a way following Sade's trail—such as infanticide—a position that has raised a number of criticisms and controversies and that paved the way for highly problematic preventive censorship in Germany. Yet, this is not the most interesting side of the issue. The side that I would like to emphasize is that Singer hides the broader human bases, and in particular the natural frameworks, that are actually at work, both in those cases in which we would like to disagree with his particular positions and those in which we would like to agree.

The very notion of interest, which applies to all those sentient persons capable of giving it a meaningful expression, is a way of hiding what it means, for us, to be born and die, and how these things might change, even radically, and create, as a consequence, a background for ever new perceptions and attitudes, which, in turn, generate the context for new moral concerns, duties and prohibitions. These broad bases of human response, these natural frameworks, are simply denied by Singer's theory. The skeptical side takes away with it the very idea according to which the world, which is a source of concerns and problems for us, is a world shaped by the texture of human responses and is the source of what is natural to us—for example, what it is for us to be born and die, and to have non-human animals among our fellows.

2.3 Kantian contractualism

Similar considerations apply to those authors of Kantian heritage who depict the moral life in terms of the respect for the moral autonomy of each person, in which the very bonds and ties to our conducts originate. Kantian contractualism derives the obligations to which we consent from our very capacity to treat each other as rational beings capable of autonomous choices: it is in fact these shared rational capacities that allow us to leave aside and do without our particular inclinations and individual constitution. The heart of this conception lies in our capacity to represent and understand ourselves as rational agents, as in the teaching of Immanuel Kant. As with utilitarianism, this line presents an inescapable source of moral concern, which in this case pertains to the respect of autonomy and to the way in which this respect influences the weight we give to our actions, not with reference to their effects in terms of goods (as with utilitarianism) but rather with reference to how they show respect for our fellow human beings and honor the duties and prohibitions at the heart of our respect (e.g., the prohibition on lying).

If utilitarianism is blind to actions and only has eyes for the causal means through which a certain good is realized, Kantian contractualism only sees actions and yet deprives them of the two aspects mentioned previously: namely, the broader human bases and their connection with the natural frameworks. Morality is accounted in terms of the deontological bonds generated from what we consent to, ruling out any source other than that of respect for the moral autonomy of others. In the picture of John Rawls, we should remain blind (the veil of ignorance) to whatever aspect and consideration fall outside our respect for each other as rational beings.[9] Hence, quite unlike utilitarianism, we have here yet another version of the exclusion of the broader framework in the light of which it is possible to understand what it would be like to respect someone, to respect a woman's pregnancy, to respect the will of a dying person. In order to understand this broader context, we should not make ourselves blind to the basis of human responses in which the respect of the moral autonomy of individuals consists—a basis that also allows us to picture how our responses (the respect for our fellow beings together with a number of other considerations) are directed toward particular human and natural circumstances, as, for example, is the case with pregnancy. Respect is only one among the many moral considerations and attitudes that we can reconstruct in light of the broader basis of human responses, perceptions, and relations; furthermore, the respect for something like pregnancy involves what pregnancy means for us, and this appeals to our very involvement with this natural framework.

As Christine Korsgaard has written, according to this picture, the rational will imposes form on the world without receiving any,[10] and this hides how the bases of the human response and natural frameworks give a form of their own to the world upon which the rational will acts. The shape they confer on the world allows us to understand what it means to respect human (and non-human) individuals in the various circumstances of life—circumstances that regulate the shape impressed on our moral considerations and also on the respect we grant to, and command from, others. Here we can appreciate some of the characteristic difficulties of Kantian contractualism, as, for example, its inability to properly make sense of, and account for, such circumstances in which one's respect cannot be directed to another autonomous person: either because there simply is no autonomous agent yet or anymore—as, for example, at the beginning of the reproductive process or at the end of life when the vital functions are lost and, with them, the cognitive capacities at the basis of rationality—or because there was never one—as with many non-human animals and with the natural environment. Martha Nussbaum raised a number of criticisms here.[11] These are situations in which the application of the Kantian contractualist picture is rather baffling or at least quite intricate, and yet what interests me, once again, are not the difficulties associated with applying this model. The aspect I am interested in commenting on is that contractualism hides the natural bases and frameworks at work both in the cases in which this approach seems inadequate and in need of a different picture that considers this broader background, *and* in the cases in which it seems to be able to account for the problematic situation at hand: for example, the respect for someone's autonomy when what is at stake is the concealing of some personal information (say, about one's medical situation), the violation of one's bodily integrity, or the threatening of the very psychological bases of self-respect. Contractualism is blind to the fact that our capacity to respect our fellow beings depends on the basis of human response through which we get in touch with the persons (or animals) in front of us.

On the contrary, from the contractualist point of view, the personal encounter with the other is exhaustively accounted for by the idea of respect that perfectly rational people owe reciprocally to each other. This idea has been defended, among others, by Stephen Darwall.[12] This is also problematic. I have claimed that the circumstances in which we show or fail to show respect for our fellow beings are grounded on bases broader than the sheer practical recognition of the rationality of those we face. That such broader bases are at work, and that respect is grounded in such bases is clearly visible in those cases when respect is denied. Let me present two emblematic cases that show the inadequacy of contractualism on this point. The first one is that of slavery as a practice kept alive in civilized circumstances, for example, in the South of the United States before the Civil War. No doubt, the way the masters treated their slaves was completely lacking in respect for their autonomy; but it is also equally clear that their way of treating them and being treated by them, of being served at the table and in some cases having secret sexual relationships with them (or genuine family relationships, as in the case of Thomas Jefferson), was made possible by a context of rich recognition of their humanity. The relationship between masters and slaves was evidently a case of personal relationship: one which recruited, in order to work, the broad basis of human responses and yet excluded the respect for the other from them. Borrowing the words of Stanley Cavell, who wrote on the matter, what was absent in the relationship between masters and slaves was the point of view of the latter, a point of view that could be seen by the masters in the eyes of the slaves.[13] To be seen from their own point of view, this very form of reciprocity, was certainly absent, and this marked their relationship as unequal. Nonetheless, the lack of reciprocal recognition did not empty their relationship of other features that make it a human and personal relationship, despite in such a tragically unjust way. The contractualist tradition does not have the resources to make this distinction, because the whole basis of human response is limited to the concept of respect and its internal logic. According to this perspective, we cannot admit that there are human responses not caught by the ideas of respect: significant responses and relations which in the case of modern slavery societies are in notable tension with the notions of respect and equality.

Another emblematic, though opposite, case of the negation of respect is that of Nazism. What the Nazis tried to do, facing many difficulties from their point of view, was to completely destroy that broad basis of human responses with reference to determinate portions of humanity. There is a clear example of this described by Primo Levi in his memoir *If This Is a Man*, which has been acutely commented on by Cora Diamond.[14] Levi describes the look that the chemist Pannwitz gave him at Auschwitz, where he was a prisoner. Levi was brought in front of Pannwitz, a chemist who was a supervisor at the factory where some deportees worked and had to decide whether to accept Levi to the factory as a chemist, hence sparing him of the terrible physical working conditions of the camp. Pannwitz sat at the desk, with Levi standing in front of him. Levi wrote how the look that passed between them "was not one between two men."[15] Here we have yet another example of the negation of respect, but we would be quite inaccurate in describing and accounting for this scene if we were to treat it as a lack of respect due to a person as a free and rational being. In Levi's example, we have the very negation of the broad basis of human responses recruited in the relationships with other people, which is present, although in the primitive and emblematic form of injustice, in the relationship between master and slave: at that moment, Levi was not seen as a human person at all.

What contractualism does not see is that treating each other as equals and autonomous is made possible by the fact that we share a broad basis of human responses, and yet it does not coincide with it. In this way, it fails to acknowledge the bases on which the idea of respect is grounded, and also fails to acknowledge the much broader range of moral attitudes that can bring us closer to each other or that might be lacking in human relationships. To consider the respect due to the rational autonomy of the other as a form of moral recognition unrelated to the broader bases of humanity—or capable of successfully accounting for them, as Darwall thinks—does not allow us to comprehend what respect amounts to, leaving the broader range of moral considerations at stake in the shadows.

2.4 Liberals and Huxley's *Brave New World*

I would now like to offer an example to illustrate this side of my criticism of both utilitarianism and Kantian contractualism. Even when these conceptions seem to hit the mark in a straightforward, undistorted way—for example, that there are such goods as happiness and the interests of persons which it is right to promote, and that there are duties that spring from the respect of the moral autonomy of persons—they hide the bases that allow us to acknowledge what we find convincing in these moral considerations: they hide the broader bases of human responses and also hide the distinctive form that these responses take in presenting us with the circumstances at stake as particular forms of human life and life in general. I take the example from Huxley's novel *Brave New World*.

In this novel, Huxley shows what it means to live in a society in which the biological facts and the attitudes toward reproduction have radically changed with respect to the society of his day in the 1930s (and ours as well). Huxley's novel is, among other things, a society in which reproduction is completely divorced from both sexuality and gestation, a society that severed all affective and intimate bonds with newborn babies, who are the outcome of social planning that includes cloning, and in which the development of the fetuses is carried out through ectogenesis. Huxley depicts a society that cultivates attitudes, perceptions, sentiments, concepts, and beliefs around this way for human beings coming into the world. In a society such as this, the very idea of being pregnant is perceived with horror and disgust. The governor Mustapha Mond describes the life of a family on Earth before the development of the new society, in the so-called "Fordian era," with the following words:

> And home was as squalid psychically as physically. Psychically, it was a rabbit hole, a midden, hot with frictions of tightly packed life, reeking with emotion. What suffocating intimacies, what dangerous, insane, obscene relationships between the members of the family group! Maniacally, the mother brooded over her children (*her* children)...brooded over them like a cat over its kitten.[16]

Linda, a woman of the new world who, because of an accident, remains confined in the savage reservoir where she eventually gets pregnant, speaks of herself in the following terms: "Turned into a savage [...]. Having young ones, like an animal."[17] The biological relationship with one's offspring is depicted as something bestial, obscene, and revolting. Huxley thus describes Lenina's reaction to her visit to the reservoir: "The spectacle of two young women giving breast to their babies made her blush and turn away her face. She had never seen anything so indecent in her life...this revolting viviparous scene."[18]

In Huxley's novel, there are a number of features that I shall not comment on—among which the presence of a vertical, top-down control of the social order, organized along hierarchical and racist principles, which makes it a representative of the important genre of dystopic novels about the totalitarian organization of society (together with George Orwell). Furthermore, the entire society is depicted as being radically deluded about reality itself: sex, which is systematically disjoined from reproduction, is depicted as a form of superficial gratification; the use of drugs is at once a form of relationship and a source of pleasure that eases one's hold on reality. These are all very interesting aspects on which I shall say nothing. What interests me here is rather the comparison we can establish between, on the one hand, the concept of assisted reproduction—criticized by the conservatives and defended by the liberals of the present time—and on the other, the concept of assisted reproduction as understood in Huxley's new world. I would like to spare, from this comparison, the other elements I have mentioned—which have to do with society in its entirety, a racist and shallow society in its most blatant features—and rather focus on the contrast between what does it mean to live with a concept of reproduction as related to the biological reproduction of the body of women and with a concept of reproduction in which this connection is completely absent. This comparison is made possible by our very capacity to imagine a world in which we find extensions and new applications of concepts with which we are familiar: this is neither a leap in the dark nor unintelligible, which would mark a rather different sort of contrast. For example, in reflecting on the sense of disgust and horror felt by the inhabitants of the new world toward viviparous human reproduction, we are called on to respond imaginatively by employing our actual sense of disgust, of which the very possibility of feeling disgust toward aspects of women's sexuality and reproduction is part—which has been historically realized in a world quite close to ours.

The point I would like to stress is that the change in factual details and attitudes, in the broad bases of human responses and in the specific form that the natural frameworks take here, makes it possible to express certain moral considerations rather than others. The sense of horror and disgust as represented in Huxley's novel is the expression of the sentiment of a perverted nature; it marks the perception that what is natural has been jeopardized, or rather overthrown. In the new world, the sense of disgust and horror is directed toward the very idea of biological reproduction. Its inhabitants perceive the viviparous reproduction of human beings as the perversion of what is natural, which depends on attitudes, beliefs, and facts: on the fact that, in such a society, human beings are not born from a woman's body. In a society where human beings are born through ectogenesis and make their sudden appearance on the threshold of society—rather than being slowly brought into it through intimate biological processes such as pregnancy—and in which this procedure is handled in a completely impersonal way, the moral problems at the beginning of life are quite different from those that we face in our societies. In Huxley's world, it is clearly not possible to reconstruct the meaning of the private character of pregnancy and birth, their intimate bond with women, and hence with their autonomy. In this context, liberals would simply lack the bases to account for their own concept of *privacy*. Fundamental goods tied to the sovereignty of women over reproduction are here clearly invisible: very simply, there is no space for them.

Huxley's novel, through the imaginative confrontation it encourages us to make, points to the broad bases of human responses and the particular natural frameworks fixing the context in which we identify and speak about women's pregnancy as the sort of process that regards the intimacy and authority of their choices. On the contrary, the perspective of utilitarians and contractualists alike hides all this from view. Yet, the thin and apparently universal concepts of autonomy and interests rely exactly on this mass of human responses woven into a context of activity considered as normal, of attitudes and factual details—we are usually born in such and such ways, which depends on a mixture of nature and technology and so forth—and hence on the particular form taken by nature—for example, the fact of being born, of being a woman. Huxley's world is populated by human beings similar enough to us. It could be even more similar if we were to imagine a society closer to us, in which this new framework for reproduction emerges from transformations (foreseeable in a not-so-distant future) that do not involve radical leaps into totalitarianism and top-down manipulations—in which individuals are treated like puppets devoid of any critical awareness of their own situation and hence of any sense of reality and measure of the depth of things. We might imagine a society in which the new conditions of being brought to life and the new attitudes associated with it emerge together with the preservation of other activities that allow us to picture these persons as endowed with a broader range of human faculties and sensibility. Now, in a society such as this, we cannot speak of the sovereignty of women over reproduction, as the conditions are simply not there anymore: the bond with reproduction is external and extrinsic. Nor do we find a place for women's interests toward pregnancy in the sense in which we now speak of the intimate interests of women over their bodies.

The very possibility of identifying something like reproductive freedom and interests as the contractualists and utilitarians depict them depends on the fact that we are beings born from the body of a woman, that pregnancy is a kind of long and complicated process which involves the body, the emotions, and the (self-)perception of women. The liberal ideal of *privacy* as it is applied to the beginning of life has a meaning because we are born in just this way. Were we to be born in a completely different way, as in Huxley's new world, we would lose the bases for discriminating a concept such as this altogether. When liberals advance their criticisms of the conservatives who reject the freedom of women and do not recognize the interests in it, they presuppose such a basis of facts and human responses: they presuppose this whole framework tied to the concept of birth. The reasons offered by liberals also refer to such sentiments and attitudes surrounding pregnancy as something intimate and precious, complex and burdensome, and always potentially dramatic that happens to women. On the other hand, their notions of autonomy and interest hide this bundle of human responses, leaving them outside the scene.

2.5 Anscombe and the conservative picture

2.5.1 *The erosion of the conservative picture*

I have shown how utilitarianism and Kantian contractualism defend interests and liberties by hiding the broader bases of human response, the bases which, for example, make reproduction, pregnancy, being a woman, and sexuality things that are the source of concerns, problems, a sense of urgency, duty, care, and attention to those individuals who exercise the full scope of their faculties. Conservatives, by contrast, craft their conceptions via the articulation of a framework against which they place the relevant moral concepts. They defend objective spaces, which are the areas of human birth, death, and sexuality, which they present as those circumstances that trigger our respect and a whole range of sentiments and attitudes—sentiments and attitudes through which we show our respect for the moral order such circumstances display and articulate. The particular kind of articulation of this framework involves the three load-bearing axes of the pre-modern ethical conceptions that I have mentioned: namely, teleology, social order, and the appeal to God.

The crucial steps of modernity have eroded these three axes, but they have done so in rather different ways. For example, thanks to notable shifts such as the establishment of modern science, the Reformation, and the new role of the subject within the social order, the course of European history has undermined a conception of divinity Kant called heteronomous, a conception that sees in the existence of a God an external guarantee of the moral order as well as of the overall cosmic order. On the one hand, what has been debunked is the very possibility of bringing all the intellectual spheres—such as those of morals, science, and the law, and not only the religious one—under the umbrella of God. Or, to put it another way, a separation has been effected between these spheres, which is a key feature of the very structure of our contemporary lives. On the other hand, these passages have brought religious beliefs within the individual conscience understood as an area of personal conviction, eroding in this way the very possibility of such beliefs performing the function of an external foundation. A deeply religious and Christian author such as Kant clearly highlights this outcome. What he introduces as the transcendental examination of the human mind shows the importance of religious ideas, and, in matters of morals, the very need to believe in God itself. However, this is no external foundation granted by religion, to the epistemological and ethical dimension of our lives in the traditional form of a metaphysical grounding usually bestowed upon these spheres, but rather a "need of reason," whereas reason is depicted as a sphere acting autonomously. This modern conception of the religious sphere—motivated, historically speaking, by the division of Europe into a multiplicity of confessions that broke the unity of Christianity apart—made it hard to keep referring to God and the Christian religion as a foundation, that is, as the framework within which to inscribe the list of duties and the entire articulation of the moral life of individuals.

Similarly, the appeal to the social order as the guarantee of the moral order has been eroded by the development of modern societies, which have witnessed the decline of intrinsic distinctions of various kinds: gender (male and female), family role (father, mother, and children), place in society (clergy, aristocracy, servant), and so forth. These distinctions, which constitute the social order, made it utterly natural to anchor our moral stance and reaction to a broader social framework: for example, to anchor the constitutive difference between male and female to the socially visible forms of female modesty and the role of male command. Social transformations—with the development of commercial society, the idea of equality, and the erosion of differences in rank—have led to the gradual formation of the modern individual with an ever greater capacity to grant herself a role and social position, and hence have progressively debunked the very idea of intrinsic social distinctions. Notwithstanding these transformative processes, society was still one of the most important sites to locate the grounds of moral life for quite a long time, though, as a consequence of the increasingly massive changes inbuilt in these processes it took the shape of *traditions* in order to refer to a cluster of endangered values and meanings.

The capacity of the teleological conception of nature to grant and secure the background in which the moral life can nestle has been equally undermined by the key passages of modern moral culture. The scientific vision has emptied the physical world of ends and essences, this being the great subject of seventeenth-century science and of the great figures of early modern philosophy. Furthermore, the weakening of the other two axes—the theological and the social ones—made it difficult for the systematical application to, and working of, teleology within the larger scheme of things. In the medieval centuries, teleology about nature could be read within the scheme of a theological creationist conception of the world and associated with an understanding of society as an organization of conducts and institutions expressive of this conception. This is at least the reading offered by the modern conservatives who, in so doing, have justified the unity of the three axes. The diverse ways of weakening the teleological conception did not, however, reduce its force and appeal, which has remained dominant if compared with the other two axes.

When considering the pluralism of religious confessions, teleology could look like an independent factor because of its operation beneath the level of human beliefs; furthermore, even when under siege, traditions still find a way to maintain their force due to the sheer power exerted over us by the past.

Facing the separation of the spheres, teleology can also claim to deal with a domain—that of action—that can claim a certain independence from the rest of nature's kingdom. In its own way, then, teleology eventually made the best of the separation of the spheres of human activity, which initially jeopardized the unified teleological framework that had held the stage in the Middle Ages. Facing the typically modern issue of accounting for the nature of the human mind as a sphere that, both in its cognitive and practical dimensions, requires concepts unlike those employed to account for the rest of nature—a problem felt by important streams of the philosophical tradition, of which Kant was certainly a leading figure, and the theme is still central nowadays—teleology and the Aristotelean account of the mind and of action can turn out to be suitable candidates once again. Free from a modern conception of nature, Aristotle describes actions as the very possibility of human nature and, at the same time, as the expression of reason, something that distinguishes human beings as unique and *sui generis*.[19] It is no surprise, then, that the teleological picture and, in the wake of it, the appeal to the social meanings of actions and traditions have been the most trodden paths of the conservative arguments.

2.5.2 The background of human life

I would here like to briefly articulate the conservative position through an examination of the views held by Elizabeth Anscombe, a first-rate philosopher engaged in a highly instructive, yet utterly desperate, task: namely, that of defending Catholicism in its entirety—she was very critical of the openings to modernity coming from the Second Vatican Council—by employing reasonable and indeed persuasive philosophical tools from the twentieth century. In a pivotal essay such as "Modern Moral Philosophy," Anscombe denounces how modern morality—and hence, at a reflective level, modern philosophical ethics—lost the very notion of a framework in which to set the crucial moral concepts, moving from the assumption that it would indeed be possible to articulate the moral life by employing such concepts as moral duty, as, for example, in its Kantian version: a concept which, however, is indeed impossible to account for without a broader theological background, in which there is a God who commands us and hence duties deriving from this command. As Anscombe writes:

> It is as if the notion "criminal" were to remain when criminal law and criminal courts had been abolished and forgotten. A Hume discovering this situation might conclude that there was a special sentiment, expressed by "criminal," which alone gave the word its sense. So Hume discovered the situation which the notion "obligation" survived, and the notion "ought" was invested with that peculiar force having which it is said to be used in a "moral" sense, but in which the belief in divine law had long since been abandoned: for it was substantially given up among Protestants at the time of the Reformation. The situation, if I am right, was the interesting one of the survival of a concept outside the framework of thought that made it a really intelligible one.[20]

Anscombe acknowledges the emptiness of the appeal to moral notions introduced as if it were possible to use them without the presence of a broader framework and presents this framework as something articulated along the three axes I have been highlighting. Before the Reformation, she writes, it was possible to refer to the theological background and divine law as the broader framework within which to inscribe and hence justify duties. Now, this path is no longer available, if not for those believing in God as the source of morals, such as the Catholics. Anscombe, then, takes into account the fact of religious pluralism. In this new framework, however, one could go back to Aristotle, who elaborated a teleological scheme independent of any religious belief. The teleological scheme offers the chance to anchor duties to the broader natural framework, to what human beings are. The teleological account of human nature displays the proper functions of the human being, together with the ends toward which her distinctive human faculties are directed. Virtues consist in the excellent exercise of these faculties directed to their proper end. In this light, Anscombe writes that, as for human beings there are a certain number of teeth that is the norm for the species, in the same vein the totality of virtues is the norm for the human species as considered from the point of view of the broader range of its faculties. The application of the teleological picture requires, according to her, notions and a use of reason that centuries of attacks on this framework by modern culture have made ever more difficult. We would in fact need to know what an action is, and this is not something we can learn from Hume or the utilitarians, or for that matter from Kant and the deontologists. An action is right when it exemplifies the kind of behavior that makes the activity in which it is involved properly human. The action may be pursued for determinate goals and with further intentions, and yet the action as such describes a human activity that we can evaluate in the light of its conformity to what is properly human.

In order to develop this picture, Anscombe helps herself with concepts and attitudes that cannot be found in the teleological scheme alone, but which need to appeal to the social meaning of actions as conveyed through tradition: the sense of reverence, modesty, the various attitudes that we can reconstruct around the various circumstances of life. As Anscombe writes elsewhere:

> Remember that we are intellectual animals, whose vegetative and animal life is part of a life framed by our intellectuality: we are nourished, for example, not like plants but like other animals, but our eating is conducted in a specially human way, reason entering into the getting and preparation of food and into the conduct of meals. Similarly our sexuality and reproduction is all tied up with our intellect, our not merely animal emotions and our aesthetic feelings. Reason and love enter into most, and certainly into all characteristically human exercise of this vital function. Hence marriage and celebration of and awe before procreation and pregnancy.[21]

The teleological argument hinges on the appeal to the social meaning of such circumstances as sexuality and pregnancy, through which it unveils the overall framework of these facts and practices. In this way, the inscription of the distinctive character of sexuality within human nature is performed not only by using a description of sexuality as aimed at reproduction but also through the reconstruction of what is properly human, which, in turn, refers to attitudes that color the sexual act and such appropriate contexts as that of marriage—contexts that can be understood and appreciated even if we do not share them due to our different upbringing or their presence in traditions of thought distant from ours. As she writes:

> For we don't invent marriage, as we may invent the terms of an association or club, any more than we invent human language. It is part of the creation of humanity and if we're lucky we find it available to us and can enter into it. If we are very unlucky we may live in a society that has wrecked or deformed this human thing.[22]

What is properly human finds expression in the distinctive ways in which we deal with human experiences, which, in turn, get signaled in our attitudes, perceptions, and language. Tradition offers a reservoir of such meanings, from which to pick in order to unfold what characterizes us as properly human, helping us in this way in the task of defining the teleological character of our actions. Therefore, the social meaning of actions helps us to articulate their teleological role and to inscribe it within a scheme that presents the various spheres and aspects of life as a coherent whole, within which Anscombe accounts for the absolute duties and prohibitions characteristic of Catholicism.

Now, what exactly is a "background" in Anscombe's perspective? It consists of everything that we do as a recognizable feature of the human way of living. Anscombe wants to defend the distinctive framework of the Catholic church, something which is clearly visible in such absolute prohibitions as the one against the murder of the innocent and those proscribing any sexual conduct different from the specific reproductive sexual act performed within marriage. With the framework of the divine law in ruins, while for those believing in God—the kind of traditionalist Christians and Jews she has in mind—it suffices to follow what God commands, the others need a background offered by the teleological apprehension of what human beings are, together with the understanding of the nature of actions described according to the social meaning attached to them traced in the relevant tradition. In this perspective, in the various domains of life, we do not respond to interests or exercise our autonomy, but rather honor what is constitutive of our humanity in these areas of life, which is revealed by the teleological argument. In this vein, Leon Kass writes: "answers depend not on science or even on ethics, but on a proper anthropology, one that richly understands what it means to be a human animal, in our bodily, psychic, social, cultural, political, and spiritual dimensions."[23] In this family of arguments, moral considerations are drawn from the description of what characterizes us within a broader human and social framework. There is an overarching framework in light of which we make moral distinctions.

The notion of a framework offers the background against which we are able to draw moral conclusions. In the picture sketched in *Modern Moral Philosophy*, we draw moral duties from the consideration of what human beings are from a teleological point of view. At the same time, we are well aware that the teleological picture finds application through the appeal to social meanings and attitudes. In this perspective, the framework represents the very foundation of ethics as is traditionally the case with the metaphysical conception: ethics is grounded in a metaphysical basis. In Anscombe's perspective, things are much more complicated since, according to her, we have lost, by and large, the framework (the metaphysics) in which ethics was grounded: we have not only lost the overall scheme of conducts, attitudes, and shared beliefs, but we have also lost the reflective level—for example, an appropriate philosophy of action and a moral philosophy, as well as a philosophy of language. The very chance to ground ethics in metaphysics then needs the rescuing of this larger picture of our life (ordinary and reflective alike) as shaped by such a framework.

2.5.3 Absolute prohibitions

As we have seen, it is important that ethics, within the specific account offered, is conveyed through absolute prohibitions, such as those pertaining to murder and sexuality. But what is the exact role of these prohibitions? Let us not forget that, in Anscombe's picture, the moral life is articulated in terms of virtues—that is, the excellent exercise of the functions that characterize us as human beings—rather than revolving around moral duties—a picture now emptied and hence useless. In the essay "Contraception and Chastity," Anscombe gives an insightful characterization of the role of absolute prohibitions. There she claims that prohibitions such as those associated with murder or sexuality, which forbid us to disgrace the human body, have to do not so much with the flourishing of human nature—the excellent thriving of the distinctive features of human beings—but rather with the very "substance of life," that is, the very concept of life whose flourishing is governed by the workings of the various virtues.[24] Absolute prohibitions mark conducts that are not simply lacking in virtue; rather they point to actions that if performed would overthrow the larger background where human action belongs and where we mutually recognize ourselves as humans and which offers the conditions to find meaning in actions and to evaluate them through the language of virtues. Absolute prohibitions mark the very confines of our humanity, if we are willing to use this turn of phrase, and hence do not merely indicate the range of operation of virtue and vice.

(This important distinction has been reprised by a number of authors, not only by conservatives. It is, for instance, central in philosophers such as Jürgen Habermas and Michael Sandel. They argue that the kinds of conducts that are now claimed to be legitimate—which Sandel questionably rubricates under the relevant notion of enhancement, and which

Habermas even more questionably extends to conducts that are nowadays completely accepted such as preimplantation genetic diagnosis—are not simply morally wrong, but are rather actions that jeopardize the very human and social framework that allows us to consider ourselves human in such domains in the first place.[25])

It has to be noticed how, according to this argument, absolute prohibitions define not so much the confines of a certain background—say, one among other possible ones—but rather of the *only* background that makes us human and hence moral beings. Anscombe does not claim to be articulating one particular background—in particular, the one defended by the Catholic hierarchies (often without good arguments, as she writes)—but is rather offering an elucidation of the only background that articulates our humanity, and that makes morals possible in the first place: a background threatened by modern moral culture as a whole. In this light, her appeal to tradition—to what we have inherited in the concepts of modesty, marriage, murder, and so on—does not refer to a determinate human texture of practices, attitudes, and language that we can compare with others (with different practices, attitudes, and concepts), but rather to how our essential human character gets exemplified. Anscombe can only admit that these concepts face corruption and eventually fall to pieces, but not that they are subject to transformation or rather encounter other concepts challenging their solidity and grounds, that is, admitting that there are other ways of weaving together life, death, and sexuality in a single rich-enough human texture.

That a change in concepts and ways of living necessarily brings about the crumbling of the entire human horizon is a thesis that we can understand and criticize if we read it as a reaction, as Mill taught us to do. Anscombe's arguments can be read in the wake of Sade and Dostoevsky. It might seem that if the background we inherited falls, from which we have received concepts such as those of modesty and marriage, then everything else will also fall: anything becomes possible and humanity itself is threatened. Now, it is true that, at certain junctures of history, the radical challenge to our ways of living and inherited backgrounds has amounted to the attempt to destroy the very bases of everything we care for—as with Nazism, for example. In the case of Nazism, as I have suggested earlier with the example of Primo Levi, it is the entire human way of living, and not only some of its specific exemplifications, that is under threat. Yet, it is deeply wrong to assimilate this case to the various examples in which what is challenged is not our common humanity but rather particular ways of living, patterns of human responses, and particular backgrounds. How could we in fact characterize human progress and civilization, if not as a challenge to established ways of living, which progressively give way to new ones, to new backgrounds, which eventually look more congenial when compared with old ones? The ease with which Anscombe—in particular, in her late essays, often addressed to a Catholic audience—brings together murder, slavery, Nazism, abortion, euthanasia and homosexuality under the same umbrella of conducts that would deny our common humanity betrays something desperate, as is the sort of Catholicism that has missed the Reformation and at the same time has remained inflexible and uncompromised. It betrays the unwillingness to acknowledge that the human texture, the background of human responses we share, has progressively included some of these activities and was transformed as a consequence of it: for example, we transformed what it means to be born, to die, and to love each other.

From conservative thinkers such as Anscombe, we can thus learn the important thesis that moral considerations are related to frameworks, and that there are moments (as with Nazism) in which what is at stake is precisely the acknowledgment of a common framework: that is, what characterizes "us" as such in the first place. What needs to be denied in these arguments is the idea that there is only one way to have a background, only one "us" available, and that the only morally relevant contrast would be that between the distinctive ways of being human as they get expressed by precise absolute prohibitions and the complete loss or corruption of our humanity. We should reject the thesis according to which the only way of being human, the only basis of human response, and the unique way of being grounded in a natural framework (to be born, die, and love) would be that constituted by the combination of the three axes, teleological, theological, and social.

At the same time as Anscombe was working on the theses advanced in "Modern Moral Philosophy," Iris Murdoch indicated an alternative path. On the one hand, their diagnoses were quite similar. Murdoch wrote, for example, that:

> it is significant that the idea of goodness (and of virtue) has been largely superseded in Western moral philosophy by the idea of rightness, supported perhaps by some conception of sincerity. This is to some extent a natural outcome of the disappearance of a permanent background to human activity: a permanent background, whether provided by God, by Reason, by History, or by the self.[26]

However, in Murdoch, the notion of a background refers to a mutable material made of the quality of the personal life and human history in its heterogeneity. As she writes:

> Philosophers have usually tended to seek for universal formulae [...]. Logic, whatever that may be determined to be, has its own universality; but when we leave the domain of the purely logical we come into the cloudy and shifty domain of concepts which men live by—and these are subject to historical change.[27]

In Murdoch's hands, the notion of a background (or a framework) allows one to bring to the surface the pluralism of moral visions in light of which we can understand people and their choices. In the wake of Murdoch's lesson, we should then make sense of the changing and pluralism of frameworks.

Modern moral culture has progressively eroded the three axes that Anscombe joints together: it has radically transformed the framework inherited from antiquity and the Middle Ages and has left us with a number of intertwined frameworks shaping the contemporary landscape together with those precious resources which, as I have been suggesting, the liberals do not seem to be able to appreciate due to their blindness toward frameworks. We can account for the various acquisitions secured in these areas of life once we leave the appeal to God behind—or if we make it our personal and creative assumption, making it a completely internal business without external guarantees; once we do without the teleological scheme, and hence stop asking what the goal is of such areas as sexuality, say, and rather reflect on what we do with them; and, finally, once we consider what we have gained by freeing ourselves from the social meanings embedded in concepts such as those of marriage, spouse, or daughter, and son. The very possibility of appreciating these changes depends on the capacity to have in view a texture of activities, perceptions, and attitudes that we simply cannot comprehend if our thought is left in the shade of the contrast between what is properly human and what is not (even if this contrast can be marked in the first place), but rather in light of the many little or not so little contrasts that open up between the various ways of conceiving and responding to the intimate union of people, reproduction, and dying. Modern moral culture left us with this plurality of frameworks, of ways of living our sexuality, being brought to life, and dying.

The acknowledgment of a plurality of frameworks brings with it the erosion of the very role of absolute prohibitions. Such prohibitions are in fact the result of the contrast between the framework of common humanity and what lies beyond it, that is, the abyss. If we grant though that moral transformations, and, in particular, what we would like to count as moral progresses, cannot be represented in terms of this contrast but rather have to do with a number of different contrasts *internal* to the space of our common humanity, then the very role played by absolute prohibitions would eventually wane, since we would not need to constantly signal the vertiginous departure from the broader confines in which human actions reside (I shall go back to this in Chapter 6, §6.1). We have to do with different types of contrasts, which we mark with different kinds of moral considerations. This is actually the situation in the various circumstances of human life. What looks artificial in the comparison between the new medical practices—for example, those tied to the request to die (assisted suicide and euthanasia)—and Nazism is that the contrast between those who welcome voluntary death and those who do not has nothing to do with the overall human framework, but rather with the contrast between particular frameworks that articulate diverse visions of the human life, visions that cohabit our common democratic space and enrich it accordingly. These visions offer a different place, meaning, and color to pain, death, personal will, and the sense of one's own dignity. They are visions that make sense of the diversified range of choices available, as, for example, the acceptance to a certain degree of the devastation of one's body caused by medical technology or the refusal of this because it is detrimental to one's personal and moral integrity. If we scale the contrast between the human background and the falling into the abyss down to its proper, peripheral dimension, and put the plurality of contrasts that characterize societies made of diverse moral visions (such as our democratic ones) back at the center, we would emancipate ourselves from the appeal and centrality of the very notion of absolute prohibitions and unlock a different level of moral considerations casting light on more important contrasts.

2.6 The liberals revisited

The conservatives react to these changes by denouncing that everything is about to fall apart, while things have only changed and are still very much in the making: this is also the thesis put forward by Albert Hirschman.[28] But the point of my critical survey of their arguments, and in particular those of a philosopher such as Anscombe, was to draw a lesson on the nature of change and hence of moral judgment. Thanks to this lesson, we can now go back to the liberals. We are now better positioned to appreciate how their arguments hide—although in a different manner from those of the conservatives—what has happened and still happens: they hide the fact that the vindication of liberties and interests is the vindication of a certain framework. The liberals are highly critical of a position such as Anscombe's. We might say, with Mill, that they acknowledge its emptiness. The liberals acknowledge that sexuality enters our lives in ways that are simply not seen by the arguments of the conservatives and that such arguments depict an empty sexual life as the world itself acting as its background has fallen. The liberals agree that Habermas's arguments—by which the practice of preimplantation genetic diagnosis transforms women and parents into child factories, and thus jeopardize what it means to be parents and the concept of reproduction itself—are indeed artificial, as they simply do not articulate the attitudes and moral thinking of the people involved. They criticize the equation of euthanasia with murder for not doing justice at all to the situation of those confined in hospitals at the end of their lives and of many other painful and tragic situations. But the liberals read no reaction in this emptiness and artificiality, that is, the typical defensive reaction of long-dead ways of living, or of only occasionally alive ones within very isolated communities, which are by now completely detached from the great streams of modernity—streams that authors such as Habermas would still like to defend and which, with greater coherence and desperation, Anscombe would like to deem as corrupted and write off accordingly. They do not see that the arguments of the conservatives should be exposed in their emptiness as they illustrate frameworks and ways of living that are simply no longer there, and *not* because we are not united and divided in our ways of living and in the frameworks that took their place—in ever new ways of understanding birth and death, marriage, and sexuality, and hence also in the relocation of these facts in different areas of human life, perhaps less central, which have eroded somewhat the solemnity of birth, death, and sexuality offering in exchange though further possibilities of movement and freedom.

Now, as regards the liberals, a different path suddenly opens up. The conservatives come up with artificial scenarios since the life they describe has simply disappeared. Anscombe, with her distinctive acuteness, is well aware that the moral life she articulates has no ground beneath it, and engages in an operation of conceptual elucidation that I have labeled as desperate, and that should perhaps be coupled with the kind of desperations and obsessions that characterize some key Dostoevskian figures, such as the Underground Man, who try to give life to a way of seeing and being that is resisted by all things common and ordinary.[29] This is how

Hume judged Pascal. But Hume, and Smith after him, opted for a too easy appeal to our alleged shared humanity, which would spare us such visions as Pascal's or, after Hume, those of Dostoevsky and Anscombe herself. And this is because what binds us might well break or change. The desperation of the strangers, of the men and women of the underground, is sometimes the struggle for a better world. We should then acknowledge how Anscombe's move goes against the grain, even if she is engaged in the defense of a contemptible worldview. Anscombe seeks reflective resources to communicate how the only world that makes us human and that allows for a moral life has long gone, and how what is alive now is hidden behind the words of the liberals but does not possess human words to be said. She tries to make us see how medically assisted reproduction, voluntary death, and the various ways of loving each other apart from traditional marriage are not only wrong but how they make us unrecognizable, as the Nazis tried to make their society unrecognizable to us.

Liberals, on the other hand, have contributed to securing new frameworks and ways of living. But their concepts are simply incapable of naming such frameworks, as they lack the very words: not because they cannot have them—which is Anscombe's thesis—but because they disown the need to have them. They do not know that they are defending not only freedom and interests, but also ever new ways of living, novel ways of being "us," creative ways of being born, dying, and loving, which make us *better human beings*. Peter Singer is emblematic in this respect. His strategy is clear: he shows the emptiness of duties and prohibitions and concludes that there is simply nothing of moral significance in the way in which we are human individuals in the diverse areas of life.[30] The path I am suggesting we take, instead, is that of acknowledging that the background has shifted and is shifting, that we are building a new conception of sexuality, one that is hospitable to subjectivity and pluralism. And so forth with other spheres of human life. The disappearance of modesty and the virtue of chastity does not signal that the bodies that constitute particular sexual experiences defended by the liberals are mere occasions for preferences. There are, of course, preferences at stake here, but they are grounded in what bodies produce (pleasures, relations, transformations of the self), and these productive capacities depend on a new background, on a new core of attitudes, perceptions, and language.

My idea is thus that to claim freedom means claiming a precise space in which it *makes sense* to choose: it means securing for oneself—as groups, societies, individuals—what sexuality, giving birth, and dying means.

Conservative thinkers have a certain idea of such a space: the space of nature, of tradition, of the divine law. The liberals do not have their own idea of such a space, but they should. It is only in terms of the transformation of frameworks, or emancipation from them and the acquisition of ever new ones, that we can make sense of freedom of choice and the promotion of individual interests.

Notes

1 David Hume, *A Treatise on Human Nature*, ed. by D.F. Norton and M.J. Norton, Oxford: Oxford University Press, 2000, Book III, Part II, Section XII, "On Chastity and Modesty." See also the essay "Of Suicide," in *Essays: Moral, Political, and Literary*, ed. by E.F. Miller, Indianapolis: Liberty Fund, 1987.

2 Donatien Alphonse François de Sade, *Aline and Valcour*, in *Marquis de Sade: Selected Writings*, ed. by T.A. Geus, New York: Dover, 2018 (abridged). In the same collection, see also *The Philosophy in the Bedroom*.

3 Fyodor Dostoevsky, *The Brothers Karamazov*, New York: Farrar, Straus & Giroux, 2002, p. 626.

4 For this expression, see e.g., John Stuart Mill, "Armand Carrel" (1837), in *Collected Works of John Stuart Mill*, Vol. XXI, *Essays on French History and Historians*, ed. by J.M. Robson, Toronto: University of Toronto Press, 1985, pp. 183–185. A contemporary author that is sympathetic to this order of explanation is Charles Taylor, who has, however, a different interpretation of Mill. See, e.g., his reflections on religion in *A Catholic Modernity?*, ed. by J.L. Heft, Oxford: Oxford University Press, 1999. For the broader philosophical framework, see Taylor, "Explanation and Practical Reason," in *Philosophical Arguments*, Cambridge (MA): Harvard University Press, 1995, pp. 34–60.

5 Jeremy Bentham, *Introduction to the Principles of Morals and Legislation*, Oxford: Clarendon Press, 1907, Chapter 2.

6 John Stuart Mill, "Bentham," op. cit., p. 80.

7 Peter Singer, *Rethinking Life and Death: The Collapse of Our Traditional Ethics*, New York: St. Martin's Griffin, 1996. For the theoretical framework, see Singer, *Practical Ethics* (3rd Edition), Cambridge: Cambridge University Press, 2011.

8 Cora Diamond, "Eating Meat and Eating People," in *The Realistic Spirit. Wittgenstein, Philosophy and the Mind*, Cambridge (MA): The MIT Press, 1991, pp. 319–334.

9 John Rawls, *A Theory of Justice*, Cambridge (MA): Harvard University Press, 1971; *Political Liberalism*, New York: Columbia University Press, 1993.

10 Christine M. Korsgaard, *The Sources of Normativity*, Cambridge: Cambridge University Press, 1996, p. 5.

11 Martha Nussbaum, *Frontiers of Justice*, Cambridge (MA): Harvard University Press, 2006.

12 Stephen Darwall, *The Second-Person Standpoint. Morality, Respect, and Accountability*, Cambridge (MA): Harvard University Press, 2006.

13 Stanley Cavell, *The Claim of Reason*, Oxford: Oxford University Press, 1979, pp. 373–378.

14 Cora Diamond, "Losing Your Concepts." *Ethics*, 98, 1988, pp. 255–277.
15 Primo Levi, *If This Is a Man*, New York: The Orion Press, 1959, p. 123.
16 Aldous Huxley, *Brave New World*, New York: Harper Perennial, 2006, p. 37.
17 *Ibid.*, p. 127.
18 *Ibid.*, p. 111.
19 On this, see John McDowell, *Mind and World*, Cambridge (MA): Harvard University Press, 1994, Lecture IV. I shall go back to these issues in Chapter 3.
20 G.E.M. Anscombe, "Modern Moral Philosophy" (1958), in *Ethics, Religion and Politics. Collected Philosophical Papers*, Vol. III, Oxford: Basil Blackwell, 1981, pp. 30–31. For an interpretation, see James Conant, "Nietzsche, Kierkegaard and Anscombe on Moral Unintelligibility," in *Religion and Morality*, ed. by D.Z. Phillips, New York: St. Martin's Press, 1996, pp. 250–298.
21 G.E.M. Anscombe, "The Dignity of the Human Being," in *Human Life, Action and Ethics*, ed. by M. Geach and L. Gormally, Exeter: Imprint Academic, 2005, pp. 70–71.
22 G.E.M. Anscombe, "Contraception and Chastity" (1975), in *Faith in a Hard Ground. Essays on Religion, Philosophy and Ethics*, ed. by M. Geach and L. Gormally, Exeter: Imprint Academic, 2008, p. 185.
23 Leon R. Kass, *Life, Liberty and the Defense of Dignity. The Challenge for Bioethics*, New York: Encounter Books, 2002, pp. 18–19.
24 G.E.M. Anscombe, "Contraception and Chastity," op. cit., pp. 187–188. Anscombe speaks of two types of virtues, which she labels as "utilitarian" and "mystic." The point of the former is "just the obvious material well-ordering of human life that is promoted if people have these virtues. Some, though indeed profitable, are supra-utilitarian and hence mystical." Chastity is a virtue "not like temperance in eating and drinking, not like honesty about property, for these have a purely utilitarian justification. But it, like the respect for life, is a supra-utilitarian value, connected with the substance of life."
25 Jürgen Habermas, *The Future of Human Nature*, Cambridge: Polity Press, 2003; Michael J. Sandel, *The Case against Perfection. Ethics in the Age of Genetic Engineering*, Cambridge (MA): Harvard University Press, 2007.
26 Iris Murdoch, "On 'God' and 'Good'" (1969), in *Existentialists and Mystics. Writings on Philosophy and Literature*, ed. by P. Conradi, London: Allen Lane, Penguin, 1998, pp. 342–343. For this reading, see Piergiorgio Donatelli, *Manières d'être humain*, op. cit., Chapter 3.
27 Iris Murdoch, "Metaphysics and Ethics" (1957), in *Existentialists and Mystics*, op. cit., pp. 74–75. See also "Vision and Choice in Morality" (1956), in *Existentialists and Mystics*, op. cit., pp. 76–98.
28 Albert O. Hirschman, *The Rhetoric of Reaction. Perversity, Futility, Jeopardy*, Cambridge (MA): Harvard University Press, 1991.
29 Fyodor Dostoevsky, *Notes from Undergrounds*, New York: Vintage Classics, 1995, pp. 12–13: "In the face of some mishaps, these gentlemen may bellow at the top of their lungs like bulls…[and] instantly resign themselves before impossibility. Impossibility—meaning a stone wall? Well, of course, the laws of nature, the conclusions of natural science, mathematics…To be sure, I won't break through such a wall with my forehead if I really have not got strength enough to do it, but neither will I be reconciled with it simply because I have a stone wall here and have not got strength enough."

30 The argument comes in two stages: it first gives science the task of describing human nature and then claims that there is nothing morally significant in our humanity so described. Peter Singer, "What's Wrong with Killing?," in *Practical Ethics*, op. cit., pp. 73 and 75: "Is it possible to give 'human being' a precise meaning? We can use it as equivalent to 'member of the species *Homo Sapiens.*' Whether a being is a member of a given species is something that can be determined scientifically," however, "the biological facts on which the boundary of our species is based do not have moral significance."

Chapter 3

Science and the space of ethics

3.1 More on the clash between liberals and conservatives

In the previous chapter I portrayed the clash between liberals and conservatives in order to highlight some selected features. Conservatives defend their moral positions by articulating a particular background. They defend a certain concept of birth, sexual life, and death. To do so, they make use of a teleological framework, which inscribes an entire moral world inside a single action—which is itself located within a precise area of life. But in order to make the teleological machinery work, they need to appeal to the social meaning of birth, death and sexuality, and hence to the fabric of attitudes, perceptions, and activities lying at the heart of those concepts. The conservatives often take a further step, as long as their interlocutor allows, which is to appeal to what God commands, which in turn ratifies what has been claimed via the reference to teleology and the social meaning of actions. In so doing, the conservatives appeal to what I have been calling the wide bases of human responses: the sheer use of right reason, on which the Thomist tradition relies, is matched with the reference to the shared fabric of attitudes and perceptions intertwined with the concepts of birth, death and sexuality. Equally, the appeal to God, when made in the relevant context of believers in a God who speaks the language of distinctive absolute prohibitions, adds up attitudes and sanctions that thicken up the very texture of this framework.

This framework leaves little space for freedom and the claim of individual interests. The liberals are well aware of this, and yet, as a reaction, they abandon the terrain of their adversaries altogether. They appeal to concepts inhabiting another level, purified of the contact with the various frameworks and ways of living, free of anthropology: for example, the point of view from the universe theorized by Henry Sidgwick, foreign to whatever particular perspective is assumed by someone, from which weighing goods and interests according to utilitarian calculations;[1] or the condition of neutrality and independence from any particular and personal condition featuring the individuals in Rawls's social contract. According to the liberals, this is the proper level from which it is possible to defend freedom and interests once for all: one from which the moral life—understood as the promotion of interests and the defense of autonomy—can be properly articulated, doing without all those conceptions and ways of living limiting it from without. And yet the liberals do not see that the level that they think they have secured is but an illusion and that what they have gained—as far as they have actually gained anything—is a movement within and along frameworks: a movement that, however, might lack the words to be said, a shift and transformation in need of conceptual articulation. The conservatives have the impression that each and every departure from their own framework means the departure from the human framework and hence the departure from morality altogether; while the liberals have the impression that the criticism of the conservative framework means the criticism of the notion of a framework as such. They are both blind to the fact that changes in history and the comparison with the present and its challenges are to be also judged in light of a shift in frameworks, in ways of living, and in the particular anthropological texture in which our activities and the circumstances of which we make experience are nestled.

On the one hand, the conservatives take circumstances such as pregnancy and reproduction as situations in which a design can be detected, in which a meaning unfolds, of which we are all witnesses (especially women), and toward which our morality can only take the form of reverence, of joy for such a gift, and of responsibility for what is taking place, which falls outside the range of choice. The density of the attitudes and sentiments surrounding these circumstances, the higher end of which we have but a glimpse of, or the will of God which we can sometimes read into them, all reveal those circumstances as being such as to leave room only for the acceptance of what is taking place. This is all connected with the relationship between women and men, with conjugal duties, and with the very meaning of sexuality. On the other hand, all the liberals see here is an area of choice, an area which involves the interests of women and couples, the prospective interests of the unborn, and all this is related to sexuality and the relationship of women with men in the context of freedom and responsibility. Liberals, though, do not see that this new perspective has not dismantled the world of perceptions and attitudes regarding the female body, pregnancy, and reproduction, and hence sexuality and the human relationships around it. This worldview is far from being dismantled. There are still women and men with bodies and with broad and deep experiences of birth, sexuality and death. These changes have progressively eroded and debunked certain attitudes, say the sense of female modesty: they have pulled to pieces an entire texture of attitudes and replaced it with another, with different perceptions of the female body, pregnancy, and all the rest—perceptions that have produced a new sense of the body and human circumstances as fraught with subjectivity and interests, ready to be individually governed in a context of mutual responsibility, relationships and care, but also of refusal and drama. A context that sees the autonomous subject entering the stage. The liberals do not realize how the natural frameworks defended by the conservatives gave way to different ones, which in turn have sometimes hosted the seeds for the creative exercise of subjectivity and the cultivation of interests. In the experience of pregnancy, sentiments of modesty and reverence have been replaced with different ones, more congenial for expressing in ever more complex ways the subjectivity of a woman's body, but also the suffering for its alterations, the engagement in the completely asymmetric relationship with what gradually grows inside of one's body. Here a scene opens that needs to be rethought as an entire texture of attitudes, perceptions and language: a scene that would make sense of reproduction in a way radically different from what was the case with the traditional background.

It is my claim that a new path for ethics opens up here. This path consists of the exploration of these new frameworks, new ways of living, and new areas of human experience in light of the moral ideas which we would like to defend. We can investigate the ways of living, and the wider frameworks hosting our life, which are more hospitable and congenial to freedom and the creative exercise of one's individual subjectivity (as I shall do in Chapter 5). My task so far has been that of unmasking the nature of the current clash between liberals and conservatives, which is also a way to read differently the history of the acquisitions of democratic societies in these areas. The result of such an operation can be taken as a new ethical departure for the liberal tradition: the latter simply cannot think of itself as moving on a level foreign to the texture of human responses and attitudes that shape what, at a determinate historical juncture, human life is in its crucial moments. With Bernard Williams, we should deflate the moralistic self-conception of liberalism as a neutral theory outside of history: a theory that does not rely on those conceptual and affective resources which form alongside with the others the common bedrock of human commitments and values.[2]

3.2 The division between ethics and science

Once this road has been taken, another question suddenly opens up. The defense of freedom and subjectivity turns out to be the defense of specific modalities in which such liberties and subjectivities take shape, and, as I have been claiming, these modalities involve what I have called the anthropological frameworks as well, as they touch on our understanding and account of birth, sexuality, and death. The defense of freedom and interests commits us to the defense of the circumstances in which we can build a particular worldview for ourselves, experiment with pleasures, and cultivate preferences that are truly ours. However, when this defense is maintained in the context of the clash with the conservatives, it might seem that the battle is merely that of debunking the conservative conceptions of human nature, to debunk their anthropology, freeing ourselves from their views on human life, by which there would be only circumstances to honor rather than opportunities to deploy our freedom and subjectivity. However, this condition blinds us toward other enemies of freedom who, unlike the conservatives, share the liberals' disenchantment with the world, to use this expression. If we think that the only battle is that of freeing human life from anthropological considerations and reconstructing morality on a completely different level, which is autonomous and detached from the anthropological one, this means leaving human life and its corollary concepts to be handled and explained by the most successful enterprise among human activities: namely, science in its various branches and the cluster of technological interventions that affect human life in light of scientific knowledge.

The conception that shifts ethics to an independent plane and leaves science the task to getting to know reality has been explicitly elaborated in the twentieth century by various non-cognitivist theories, and in particular by neo-positivist conceptions, which have variously defended the independent space occupied by moral thought with respect to the epistemic dimension of our investigations and in particular to the scientific one.[3] It has been claimed that, on the one hand, in accordance with modern science, there are no ends and essences in nature, and more generally there simply are no entities bearing any moral significance; while, on the other, that our moral criteria do not respond to nature but rather to independent principles operating on a different plane. There are no domains of nature to be honored, but rather natural processes to be explained only, with independent moral criteria belonging to a different plane such as autonomy and the promotion of interests.

The Kantian tradition has elaborated its own version of the fact-value dichotomy, which is different from the one defended by non-cognitivism. In their own way, the Kantian conceptions are in need of an idea of the world in which the moral will is operative, which is not the world known and investigated by the sciences. However, this idea is sufficiently thin—it is noumenic indeed—to actually leave the world in the hand of the sciences. Contrarily to the motives at the heart of this perspective, the solution to the problem of the *sui generis* feature of rational subjects, which locates them outside the empirical order, eventually leaves the grasp of the world to the scientific enterprise and gives no explanation as to how moral thinking affects the world by transforming it: the moral world is punctiform and is revealed only at the moment of choice, leaving all the rest in the hands of science.[4]

The separation of ethics from nature had the following effect. Moral criteria had to be elaborated independently from the consideration of human nature; however, they get applied to situations of life to which the sciences (medical-biological and social alike) have privileged access, and hence they end up being slaves to these perspectives. In light of this, autonomy and the promotion of well-being are criteria whose footing relies on how the biological and social sciences picture human life. If we highlight this further line running through our modern culture, we are in a position to acknowledge how the conservatives are not the only enemies of freedom and the search for subjectivity, since the ways in which science and technology have taken over the concepts of human life for their own ends equally represent a potential peril.

Such ends are indeed admirable for the large part, as they are variously tied to the pursuit of knowledge and to intellectual curiosity, beyond their interest for the improvement of our life conditions and their thirst for ever new theoretical and practical discoveries to be put at the service of humanity. The defense of freedom and subjectivity also and primarily involves the defense of the scientific and technological developments of humanity, which further knowledge in ever new directions, broaden our possibilities of choice, improve our life conditions, give rise to transformations in society, and represent occasions of freedom and happiness. However, these are ends shaped by that particular kind of activity: namely, the enterprise of knowledge in its various branches and specific technological ventures. They are ends shaped by them, rather than by the primary moral labor, if I may use this expression, which consists in giving form to one's life in a free, creative, and happy manner. If we let science and technology be our only guidance for the various departments of human life, we would greatly impoverish our relationship with them and jeopardize the very bases of the ethical life. From the deep and rich viewpoint of ethical subjectivity, we have every interest in the development of science and technology; it makes no sense to advance a general criticism of these activities and their goals. The criticism is rather directed at the idea that these epistemological and technological ends *exhaust* the experience in the areas of human life which is relevant in order to properly reflect on our existence and to engage in the ethical investigation of freedom and happiness.

Now, this is exactly the path suggested by those significant lines within our modern moral culture that have blinded themselves to what the stakes are in their own criticism of the conservatives and of their anthropological visions. They thought, and still think, that the task is that of moving away from the level of human experience in these areas of life—the anthropological level—so as to reach a different and independent plane; furthermore, they are convinced not only that it is possible to leave the reflective and practical labor in these areas of life to science and technology, but also that it should be the case as doing so is indeed a key element of their battle. According to the line of thinking I have been proposing, this way of seeing things is utterly inadequate. If we leave the ethical task of thinking in terms of freedom and interests unguarded and detached from the reflection on the specific anthropological ways in which such liberties and interests take shape, we would base these ethical forms on grounds on which we have not properly reflected, leaving them in the hands of the goals envisioned by science and technology. On the other hand, if we question which are the natural frameworks more hospitable to freedom and the creative exercise of subjectivity, we are in a position to critically reflect on how science and technology have taken over these areas of human life. This is indeed another side of the story, different and separated from the criticism of the conservatives, which should be taken into consideration.

3.3 Science and human life

Let us take a step back. The traditional conceptions defended by the conservatives represent human life, in the three ways I have indicated, as a site of meanings to honor rather than as an occasion to give shape to one's subjectivity. The various spheres of human life are woven together by this horizon of attitudes, perceptions and activities characterized by radical asymmetries. Religious practices, intimate bonds, and the relationship with the authorities are all moments in which the relations among persons— which, after Foucault, we can consider as power relations[5]—generate the pregnant body, sexuality, and dying as ways of being, as forms of experience, in which individuals give shape to themselves. Our being individuals is shaped by forms of experience that make us so in the form of a conformation to a design, to meanings, to the dictates of priests, fathers and authorities. The entire scene is shaped by the kind of relations and attitudes, and hence no one is free from them, not even those standing on the other side of the relation of power, such as the father or the priest. In a climate such as this, writes Mill with reference to the family, everybody is shaped by these forms of experience.[6]

Now, this is a scene that produces its own peculiar kind of goods, which has to do with the dimension of conformity, acquiescence and obedience. These are the goods tied to the acceptance of reality as something which is not in our hands, the goods of caring in radically asymmetric forms, of blind loyalty and trust, exactly because such goods are not grounded in relations between peers. These are, for example, the relations depicted in some of the movies by Lars von Trier, such as *Breaking the Waves* (1996) and *Dancer in the Dark* (2000), movies that are equally fascinating and disturbing, I believe, also because they invite us to face forms of obedience and acceptance so pure and far from the values of autonomous subjectivity as to become hideous and disquieting. The life shaped by these forms of experience allows for movements, but these are punctiform movements, as they represent small temporary turns: these are the moments in which an act of resistance (once again in Foucault's technical usage of the term[7]) takes place, moments in which one's subjectivity emerges in the attempt to claim back what has been extorted from us anyway—for example, in the pleasure one might experience in obedience or conformity claimed as one's personal possession. In conforming we are giving form to our life in a way that is, if only negatively, in the first person. In the end, it is in fact us, those who conform, who live such experiences: the pleasure of obedience, of absolute fidelity, of a care free of reciprocity, acknowledged as ways of affirming ourselves.

I went back to the ways of life defended by the conservatives in order to signal how what turns the areas of human life into forms of experience, into anthropological frameworks which shape the entire intellectual and moral life,—even the one inhabiting the higher stores, such as those populated by thin and apparently universal concepts—what makes them capable of shaping life in this way, is the complex fabric of attitudes, perceptions, activities, and relations among people. I would now like to add that the epistemological and practical dimensions tied to the sciences have the power to weave in their own way this fabric of considerations that generates forms of experience capable of shaping an entire life. If we follow Foucault, we are actually encouraged to read a rather strong continuity of modes and techniques into the apparent discontinuity which characterizes the history of the most intimate aspects of human experience, as, for example, in the passage from the traditional forms of control typical of Christianity to the forms of discipline tied to the new human sciences such as psychiatry and institutions such as hospitals. The various perversions which psychiatric knowledge lumped together in its nineteenth-century categories, now perceived as comical, to a certain point though, with practical outcomes in courts of law, in the social life of people, and in the very perception which people had of themselves—is the result of the thickening of practices and attitudes about specific areas of life, which furthers in different ways the work of Christianity and its diverse churches, and in particular the Roman church: the kind of work—or better the combination of relations, perceptions, attitudes, and language—in which certain areas of life are shaped by forms of cognitive and practical interests aimed at unveiling the truth in them, reporting them to someone, or controlling them for higher interests. Foucault tells a fascinating story of some such forms of this continuity within the discontinuity between confession, made so very central in counter-reformation Catholicism, and the sciences of the truth of the soul such as psychiatry and psychoanalysis.[8]

Foucault's point generalizes, however, and as such, it is open to rather diverse explanations. The forms of knowledge and technology tied to the sciences in their applied dimensions—that is, medicine, but also the social sciences working on individual conducts whose results offer the ground for public policies, such as the policies of risk associated with food or sex, drugs policies, and family policies—shape areas of human life with reference to this collection of interests: interests to know as well as interests to intervene. Foucault has shown us quite convincingly that the simple interest to know is not neutral at all, it is not free from moral and human significance. To conceive, for example, sexual experience as having the shape of a discovery of something about oneself and others is quite different from conceiving it, say, as an interest in giving oneself and others pleasure[9]. We are now well aware that, in this field, the preoccupation to know in order to cure is a rather suspect exercise, and actually betrays a scene which is quite easy to expose as moved by an interest to shape and control, in which knowledge turns out to be an instrument of control of others over us. But the point also applies to those areas which appear as rather innocuous, as, for example, the interest to better understand a disease, its nature and development, so as to effectively address it. In this case as well, it is far from innocent to think of a disease exclusively in light of these epistemic and practical interests, as this would leave out other interests which might well shape these areas of life, here understood as areas of the most diverse experiences.

An emblematic example is that of cancer, which allows the bringing together of some of the threads I have been spinning so far. Cancer is a disease surrounded by a great number of painful and oppressive meanings, and it might seem that the only interest which we might nurture in its respect is that of knowing it in order to prevent and cure. The meanings it carries with it are usually understood as the residue of a world in which cancer (like other pathologies) was not treated simply as a disease, but rather as the expression of a larger scheme in which sentiments of blame and shame were deep-set. In this light, the liberal conception sketched previously might look like a very promising alternative because of its emphasis on the need to empty human life of meanings and handing it, on the one hand, to science and, on the other, to independent moral criteria, which in this particular case have good reasons to affirm the interests of medicine. Therefore, this seems to be a positive test for the view that promotes the liberation from received anthropological conceptions: it frees human life from the meanings that have thickened into it and hands it over to science, leaving moral criteria to dictate their own interests.

However, this view is inadequate. It, in fact, leaves out the key dimension of our experience with illness, for example, with cancer, which patients undergo in the first person: an experience full of meanings and thoughts, a texture of perceptions and attitudes which meets with what doctors say and do, but which is distinct from it and much wider in scope. It is from within this form of experience that the liberals dismiss the meanings built into the tradition, the blame and shame which surface in our thinking and talking about cancer—where a heart attack is perceived as a good death, while cancer is poisoned with negative metaphors—in order to claim a different form of experience in the first person which they are making of their illness. The criticism of the characteristic meanings pertaining to the traditional framework within which illness is easily read as a form of divine punishment, as a disorder in the teleological design; the criticism of the social meaning of illness as a stigma; the criticism of the ways illness is intertwined with meanings following the three axes I presented; the sharp criticism advanced by Susan Sontag in her well-known book:[10] these should not be understood as a criticisms addressed to the entire form of the personal human experience of illness, which should give way to the experience with illness as it has sedimented into the medical gaze, knowledge, and techniques. Rather, it should be read as a criticism now raised by patients against forms of experience in which there seems to be little space to freely claim one's subjectivity.

In this light, the form of experience which has thickened around medicine can also be said to be constraining, as it too leaves little space for subjectivity. It shapes the areas of human life from the point of view of the medical gaze, of the epistemic and practical interests to cure. It is not a way to shape the experience with illness which allows for the articulation of this experience in the first person, as something lived and explored by every single individual. We should not mount an opposition between the interest in subscribing to the goals of medicine in this and other fields, and the interest in producing a notion of illness—say, cancer—which resists the monopolization of such interests so as to remain open to the subjective movements of single individuals. If we engage in a fight for freedom and subjectivity in these areas, it is simply unthinkable that this fight should not aim to the thickening of forms of human experience that allow one to face illness in personal ways, in light of a plurality of orientations, of ways of reacting to pain, to what happens to us and which we can control only partially or very little indeed, to the fragility and vulnerability of our body, and to the fact of death. The traditional framework loaded these experiences with fixed meanings and attitudes with no space left for freedom, while we now have the chance to turn these experiences into occasions for a personal path of self-transformation which can be touched by a variety of meanings and attitudes, a rich plurality of attitudes toward life.

The dominant liberal picture I am criticizing is blind to this wealth of materials through which we give shape to the personal and unique feature of our self and shifts the exercise of freedom and subjectivity elsewhere, on a plane where choice cannot be so shaped by these experiences, cannot be nurtured and informed by the knowledge of this material. At the same time, however, these areas of life have become the fieldwork of knowledge and technologies, such as the medical ones, giving them a form according to their own principles and assumptions. The sense of distress and conflict felt by patients toward medical treatments that neglect the personal and spiritual dimension of diseases betrays the inadequacy of this approach. These patients would like to experience their own illness in the first person but may not find the words and conceptual space to do so as medical practice is not in a position to help. At the same time, even if they have religious beliefs, they often find the religious point of view inadequate since they see it as part of a world which was equally blind to the possibility of having an experience of illness in the first person. Their distress and their voices point to the direction which, I believe, should be taken as a society, as professions, as groups, and as individuals: namely, that of thickening up spaces of experience such as these, that is, spaces in which illness is a modality of the creative exercise of one's self, even if only in the asymmetrical form that has to do with dealing with something we so painfully endure.

This form of experience represents the basis on which we can sensibly form desires, dispositions, and preferences in light of which to rethink medical practice. The liberal concepts of autonomy and interests should find here the source of the respect for the autonomous will of the patient and of the duty to promote her interests. The choices belonging to the sphere of the relationship between doctor and patient, and in particular the delicate and crucial choices at the end of life, can be regarded as choices springing from one's subjectivity and faithfully representing it only to the extent that such choices had the chance to shape themselves by taking medical reality in and not by being dethroned by it. This is exactly what happens if we consider these choices—for example, the request of informed consent, or the request of withdrawal of treatment—as coming from a self who inhabits a reality alien to her.

I advance this general diagnosis of the areas of life I am investigating. I have spoken of cancer and illness, but we should defend this approach in all the crucial areas of human life, in reproduction, sexuality, and dying. The two conceptions I examined proved to be equally inadequate. The first one because it puts the areas of human life in the hands of traditional conceptions, of their representatives, and their power over our bodies and the intimate substance of our self, but also in our own hands as long as we let ourselves be shaped by the roles inscribed in the traditional framework, such as those of the father, husband, wife, and so on. (The possibility to passively receive given forms of experience without feeling the need to reflect and to give our experience a personal form is greater in traditional roles such as those belonging to the family than in those that are more open and explorative.) The second one is also inadequate because, as we have seen, the scientific-technological conception—whose goals are so precious to us and whose distinctive modality of experiencing represents one of the highest uses of our human faculties—is usually taken to be the privileged or even the only viable one to access these areas of human life—ruling out other equally precious sources of interest and modalities of experience.

3.4 The quarrel over scientific naturalism

The criticism of those conceptions which see in science and technology the privileged modalities of access to human life I have been outlining in this chapter is part of a heterogeneous critical line. This line can be shared by those positions engaged in showing the inadequacies of modern culture. The views endorsed by Anscombe and Kass are of this kind. There are also lines of thought that, moving from Heidegger, offer an account of modernity that are quite critical of the modalities of access to life mediated by technology and science, despite, in this case, the diagnosis being different as it reaches way back to the unfortunate beginnings—by their lights—of our culture in Greek thought.

What I want, rather, to show is the importance of other lines of thought that offered a diagnosis along paths congenial to the one defended in this book. On the one hand, there is a line we might label as Kantian, a line that finds a congenial embodiment in Wittgenstein and is intertwined with the contemporary reprise of Aristotle's stances. Anscombe herself is also a crucial figure in this line. In this line of thought, whose most renowned positions are those of Hilary Putnam and John McDowell, the criticism is not raised against modern thought and its pivotal components such as the scientific enterprise, but rather against the very idea according to which the scientific enterprise in its various dimensions represents an exhaustive approach in the light of which it is possible to make sense of the entire range of human experience.[11] Our human activities,—perceptual, cognitive, emotional and practical—the varieties of encounters of mind and world, the encounter with other people, deliberation and action: these are all aspects which make us the kind of natural beings we are, and this fact re-fashions a concept of nature that is *not* the one handed to us by science. We need this different notion of nature and reality in order to make sense of the broader reach of human activities.

This line of thought can be profitably related to a different one, which has been independently elaborated by Foucault. In his course *The Hermeneutics of the Subject*, Foucault defended the idea by which modernity should be accounted for as the establishing of a paradigm that eventually strangled the transformative and constructive capacities of subjects, one that represents reality as a given, a paradigm that obscures our active contribution in the making of the concept of reality which is the very object of scientific inquiry.[12] In the ancient world, according to Foucault's account, knowledge was not so much aimed at unveiling reality but rather at transforming the subject, and in this light, reality becomes what a subject so transformed has access to. In this perspective, it is not so much science but rather the establishing of the theological picture, in its distinctive Thomistic variety, that brought about the rupture which conceals the internal relation between knowledge and subjectivity, presenting knowledge as a way into reality which does not call for the transformation of the subject.[13] The possibility of making science the privileged modality of access to the world, whose adequacy is a function of its independence from idiosyncratic partialities, represents a later moment of the path opened by the theological framework.

In Foucault's perspective, the access to reality granted by science is itself the outcome of a particular kind of transformation of the subject. The idea of privileging this modality of access to reality represents a reinforcement of the same kind of concealment and hence appears as utterly inadequate. In representing reality as something out there awaiting explanation, the scientific worldview strengthens the theological picture that first encouraged us to see reality as something independent from, and external to, the subject. What Foucault is offering is indeed a form of unmasking. We can picture science differently, that is, as an activity that is the outcome of the education of the self, of a transformation of her faculties, of a discipline aimed at the realization of a certain concept of reality. In this light, if we start to reflect on the concepts of freedom and the good life, we simply cannot rely on this notion of reality or the notion of reality handed to us by the theological picture, but we should rather reach back to the broader capacities for transformation of the subject and ask ourselves, from that point of view, what knowledge transforms the subject, neither in order to turn her into a faithful sheep in the hands of the spiritual pastor nor to make her a reliable inquirer of nature but rather to make her free and happy.

These two critical lines—the one issuing from Wittgenstein and the one opened by Foucault—are quite important for my own perspective. In my view, to freely exercise one's subjectivity and have interests of one's own is a matter concerning the possibility for specific ways of being oneself in the various spheres of life: as women with respect to pregnancy, as individuals endowed with a certain sexuality, vulnerable in their bodies and whose prospect is at one point their death. I have claimed that the ethical question should be raised in the following terms: what are the specific, anthropological, conditions of the exercise of freedom? In this light, the two perspectives—the traditional one and the one that privileges science and technology—are both enemies of freedom to the extent that they defend specific ways of life and forms of experience which are not aimed at the shaping and realization of one's subjectivity but are rather independent of such movements. The way out I have indicated is that of going back to primary human potentialities, to the possibility of giving shape to the various spheres of life, to one's nature and hence to the reality we experience, in ways that are the most congenial to freedom.

In order to access these primary potentialities, following the lead of the two lines sketched above could be of help. The Wittgensteinian line highlights how the concept of human nature capable of making sense of the broadest range of human activities is not the one shaped by scientific interests but rather the one we employ when we examine the character of these activities—an examination which requires acquaintance with them rather than the repudiation of this acquaintance and the embracing of the detached point of view of the scientist or an alleged point of view *from nowhere* (to use Thomas Nagel's picture and turn of phrase).[14] But it is equally important to learn from the other line explored by Foucault, according to which the primary potentialities are illuminated by the knowledge and techniques capable of activating them. The scientific point of view is itself the outcome of a particular form of education of the human faculties. We can ask, and, as a matter of fact, this was indeed Foucault's question: what are the modalities of education of the self that transform us into subjects capable of living with freedom and interests springing from our very subjectivity?

This perspective allows us to take an original stand in the old quarrel over scientific naturalism. After having witnessed, for a number of decades in the twentieth century, the qualified affirmation of the view that granted culture and the humanistic disciplines privileged access to the unlocking of reflection on society and its individuals, a different assortment of views now prevails that puts the methods and results of the various sciences at the center, especially those furthering the evolutionary framework. For one thing, the defense of these naturalistic perspectives allows for the criticism of the grounds of traditional and religious conceptions. This explains, among other things, how part of those critical of the privilege accorded to science are the conservatives in their crusade against modernity, such as the authors in the line advanced by Anscombe. However, as I have been suggesting, we can rethink the very terms of the debate. We can mount a criticism of the privilege granted to science without turning this criticism into the defense of conservative positions, but rather as part of a different program through which elaborating and defending those positions supporting freedom and subjectivity. In this perspective, both the traditional positions and those granting a privilege to science and technology, even if motivated by different reasons, deprive individuals of the resources to shape the space of their subjectivities, of their interests, and of their very freedom. On the other hand, once these bases have been reconstructed, we are in a position to appreciate the role played by science and technology not only within the limits of their access to reality but also acknowledge how this kind of access to reality can nurture in seminal and crucial ways the wider experiential basis of scientists and technologists. Foucault spoke of the figure of the "specific intellectual" in order to indicate the value of the wide-ranging human experience in a broad sense ("political," as he labels it) gained from the specific point of view of a certain profession, tied, for example, to her specific scientific and technological competences.[15]

For this reason, the present contrast between science and religion or between science and teleology is utterly inadequate. We need the broad experience of things and life that none of these dimensions is in a position to account for. Traditional conceptions, for example, those appealing to God or to a teleological framework, aim at accounting for a notion of human nature faithful to human interests and needs, but they do that in a way that departs from the crucial teaching of modernity: namely, the centrality of the individual and her subjectivity. The traditional framework, as we have seen, leaves no space for subjectivity and individual interests. Our task nowadays is that of elaborating conceptions and natural frameworks which speak a human language, but the language of a humanity which in the meanwhile has secured the form of the individual life, of the subjective life, in crucial spheres such as those of birth, sexuality and death. In this light, the neo-Aristotelean philosophical programs—shared in diverse ways by authors engaged in responding to the problems of Kant and Wittgenstein about the character of the framework that articulates the very conditions of possibility of the human mind and of its various activities—do not see that, in the meanwhile, this basis has been transformed, making room for the centrality of the individual and her subjectivity.[16]

Yet, there is a further issue at stake. If we acknowledge that our inquiry is aimed at those primary human potentialities capable of nourishing forms of freedom and subjectivity, we also see how such primary human potentialities are modalities of self-transformation, ways of activating faculties, ways of educating and remodelling the self—which in the end is Foucault's main point in *The Hermeneutics of the Subject*. To think of them in terms of the mobility of the self and of its capacity to transform itself is a lesson that simply cannot be drawn from the traditional metaphysical framework, Aristotelean or Thomist alike. It is no mistake that Foucault considered Aristotle as the big exception in classical culture—which, in his reading (shared by Pierre Hadot), was engaged in the delineation of forms of knowledge and techniques aimed at the transformation and care of the self—and considered Aquinas and the scholastics as mainly responsible for the establishing of the theological framework which almost managed to strangle once and for all the perspective of the mobility of the self—while the latter finds an alternative outcome in the Augustinian spiritualist tradition, even if it is equally at the services of the specialized interests of Christianity to discipline and subject rather than to create spaces for freedom and subjectivity.[17] The need to reflect on the primary human potentialities calls for the notion of the mobility of the self, which represents another motif critical of the metaphysical line. To think of the shape taken by the anthropological space of freedom requires to acknowledge how such space is the result of knowledge, techniques, and activities which transform the self, working on its faculties. This possibility of transformation of the self is, however, hidden both in the metaphysical-theological and in the Aristotelian-teleological frameworks and in that which grants science and technology the privileged access to reality.

In this chapter, I have highlighted a number of motives in the light of which it is possible to appreciate how some crucial clashes shaping the landscape of contemporary culture are indeed poorly equipped to account for the need for freedom and subjectivity. The clash itself between conservatives and liberals is inadequate, being a version of the clash at the heart of modernity between traditional conceptions and champions of Enlightenment and of scientific and democratic modernity. Yet the clash between traditional conceptions—for example, in the form of religious thinking—and scientific naturalism is equally inadequate. What is missing from these various contrapositions is what I think is the fittest candidate if we care for the defense of freedom and subjectivity. Freedom and subjectivity are only possible as specific forms expressed in modes of life, conceptual landscapes made of activities, perceptions, attitudes, and relationships among people. We need to be able to glimpse the possibility of these landscapes, to see them as modalities of self-transformation. The traditional and conservative conceptions in the various versions I have presented offer a picture of these landscapes that rules out freedom and subjectivity altogether; liberals and scientific naturalists are blind to these landscapes and hence miss their importance entirely. We should properly focus on them, cast some critical reflection on them, and ask in this light what the freedom and the spaces of subjectivity we are interested in defending consist of.

Notes

1 Henry Sidgwick, *The Methods of Ethics*, Indianapolis: Hackett, 1981, Book III, Chapter XIII, § 3. For an application, see Peter Singer, "What's Wrong with Killing?," in *Practical Ethics*, op. cit., p. 90: "Is it speciesist to judge that the life of

a normal adult member of our species is more valuable than the life of a normal adult mouse? It is possible to defend such judgments only if we can find some neutral ground, some impartial standpoint from which we can make the comparison." Singer goes on defending this point of view in the pages that follow.

2 Bernard Williams, "In the Beginning Was the Deed," in *In the Beginning Was the Deed. Realism and Moralism in Political Argument*, Princeton: Princeton University Press, 2005, pp. 22–23.

3 For a criticism see Hilary Putnam, *The Collapse of the Fact/Value Distinction and Other Essays*, Cambridge (MA): Harvard University Press, 2002.

4 These pictures and the criticism they pose to the Kantian moral line have been elaborated by Iris Murdoch. See, for example, Murdoch, "The Idea of Perfection" (1964), in *Existentialists and Mystics*, op. cit., pp. 299–336.

5 Michel Foucault, *The History of Sexuality*, Vol. 1: "An Introduction", London: Allen Lane, 1979.

6 John Stuart Mill, *The Subjection of Women*, op. cit., pp. 293–295.

7 Michel Foucault, *The History of Sexuality*, Vol. 1, op. cit., pp. 95–97.

8 Michel Foucault, *Abnormal. Lectures at the College de France 1974–1975*, ed. by A.I. Davidson, New York: Picador, 2004.

9 Michel Foucault, *The History of Sexuality*, Vol. 1, op. cit.

10 Susan Sontag, *Illness as Metaphor*, New York: Farrar, Straus & Giroux, 1978; *Aids and Its Metaphors*, New York: Farrar, Straus & Giroux, 1989.

11 Hilary Putnam, *Reason, Truth and History*, Cambridge: Cambridge University Press, 1981; Hilary Putnam and Martha Nussbaum, "Changing Aristotle's Mind," in Hilary Putnam, *Words and Life*, ed. by J. Conant, Cambridge (MA): Harvard University Press, 1994, pp. 22–61; John McDowell, *Mind and World*, op. cit.

12 Michel Foucault, *The Hermeneutics of the Subject: Lectures at the Collège de France 1981–1982*, ed. by A.I. Davidson, New York: Picador, 2005. Foucault introduces the notion of spirituality in order to represent the relationship between subject and truth: "[Spirituality] postulates that for the subject to have a right of access to the truth he must be changed, transformed, shifted, and become, to some extent and up to a certain point, other than himself" (p. 15). For the overall picture, see the entire lecture of January 6th 1982.

13 *Ibid.*, p. 21.

14 Thomas Nagel, *The View from Nowhere*, New York: Oxford University Press, 1986.

15 Michel Foucault, "Entretien avec Michel Foucault" (1976), in *Dits et écrits, II, 1976–1988*, Paris: Gallimard, 2001, pp. 140–160.

16 Apart from Anscombe, see also Philippa Foot, *Natural Goodness*, Oxford: Clarendon Press, 2001. An author who explicitly tackled this issue is Martha Nussbaum. See e.g. Nussbaum, *Love's Knowledge. Essays on Philosophy and Literature*, New York: Oxford University Press, 1990.

17 Michel Foucault, *The Hermeneutics of the Subject*, op. cit., p. 17: "As everyone knows, Aristotle is not the pinnacle of Antiquity but its exception." On the relationship with Hadot and Cavell, see the writings of Arnold I. Davidson, e.g., "Ethics as Ascetics: Foucault, the History of Ethics, and Ancient Thought" (1994), in *The Cambridge Companion to Foucault. Second Edition*, ed. by G. Gutting, Cambridge: Cambridge University Press, 2005, pp. 123–148.

Chapter 4

Frameworks

4.1 The frameworks of thought

In this chapter I would like to deal with the very notion of framework, or background, and the idea of reality deriving from it. What I have been doing so far is to highlight contrasts— between the supporters of the pre-modern world and those of modernity, between conservatives and liberals, and between scientific naturalists and anti-naturalists. The notion of a background has surfaced from the presentation of these clashes. In the clash between liberals and conservatives, the notion has surfaced as the cluster of facts, activities, perceptions, attitudes, and relations which give life to a way of being individuals in the various areas of human life—ways unacknowledged by the liberals and recognized by the conservatives in a modality which rules out any other configuration. Frameworks have surfaced as such cluster of facts and relations of this kind among individuals that generates entire conceptual dimensions, for example, those surrounding birth, sexuality, and death. Backgrounds represent the basis of our experience, and, in this light, they provide the conditions for our thinking in these areas. I have shown how this is of crucial importance for understanding the standpoints of the two competing parties. The liberals have the impression of shifting to a different level, while their capacity to account for and defend such things as reproductive freedom depends on attitudes, perceptions and facts that constitute a certain framework of reproduction, a framework that shapes this conceptual dimension in distinctive ways. In Huxley's new world, different facts and attitudes constitute a framework that is completely unlike ours, in light of which we are unable to see what the liberals defend in our actual world: the citizens of the new world would have to engage in an imaginative effort in order to be able to visualize our values, and they would eventually read them as the expression of our frameworks. The conservatives, by contrast, defend particular frameworks that are hospitable to the values they champion, but they think that this is the only possible way of granting the anthropological conditions of possibility for thinking about human beings and their activities, and about good and bad.

Examining this clash helps us to bring into focus the notion of framework which delineates the conditions of our intellectual and practical movements in the world, and in particular, in the various areas of human life—a notion that introduces these conditions as concrete factors, forms of experience that have been thickening in history and made possible by all sorts of facts about the world and ourselves. In this regard, I would like to underline two aspects: 1) our experience and the thinking about it are shaped by particular frameworks anchored to the world and history; 2) these frameworks appear as horizons in which thought progresses with a certain degree of freedom: they shape it and grant it a specific aspect and color, and yet they do not limit it within fixed borders.[1]

These are the bases that make experience and thought possible, which are mobile in character and can take directions that are for the most part not given in advance: they depend on the encounters that experience and thought make with reality and hence are up to us entirely. However, there are cases of frameworks that are so corrupted, so permeated by activities and conceptions that do all that is in their power to keep out of reach the mobile and free aspects of experience and thought, to become almost unchangeable and immobile.

In this perspective, then, the movements of thought through which we reflect on our experience and check it in its moral dimension are shaped by frameworks. In the scheme of things I have been sketching, the liberals disown the relationship between moral thinking and frameworks, and picture the former as completely free: the utilitarians make it hinge on the consideration of interests that, while originating in experience, do rely on an extremely thin notion of experience free of any concrete foothold in life; the contractualists make it operate in the void in which the rational will operates, constrained only by the respect for the rationality of our fellow agents and not by the matter that comes from the concrete base of our lives. The conservatives acknowledge in their own peculiar way the relation between moral thinking and frameworks, as they ground ethical thinking in the description of its natural bases, but they disown this very feature of such bases. They take them into consideration in order to find in them some essential order and get rid of what does not fit in such an order. As Alasdair MacIntyre wrote quite clearly, in the ancient Aristotelean framework and then in the medieval one, the fundamental distinction was between how human beings could be if they realized their essential nature and how they happen to be in their contingency.[2] This allows the various signature moves of the conservatives that we have seen: they identify selected aspects of human nature as crucial in order to offer an account of the human framework and, when these aspects eventually have faded away—for example, teleology, the social meanings inbuilt in human nature, and the divine law—argue that the framework has shifted in such ways that humanity itself, and with it, the very possibility of the moral life, eventually are jeopardized. The conservatives, in short, do not acknowledge how the bases of ethical thinking hinge on contingent facts, on activities, history, and human relations, which go to shape the scene of thought, to grant it a determinate aspect, to generate conceptual dimensions such as a certain concept of birth, a certain concept of sexuality, and a certain concept of death, with such bases remaining mutable nonetheless, hence generating an order that is equally mutable. Furthermore, as I have claimed, they do not acknowledge how, within a determinate framework, it is possible to glimpse an alternative order or at least small turns or even only singular moments of resistance.

As a consequence, it can be said that thought possesses a freedom of its own—a mobility of its own. Some may find their way within the conceptual dimension of birth and death, gaining the capacity to picture them in different ways, to apply them differently: a freedom which may eventually be able to make sense of the old fashioned concepts of birth and death in utterly novel circumstances. Change, transformations, and what we might regard as improvement or decline, depend both on the movements of the backgrounds and on the movements of thought. But we are now in a position to acknowledge that thought itself is a way of picturing an aspect of what it means to have a framework. What I am calling thought is the reflective component—with multiple realizations and in a variety of degrees—of having a framework. For example, a certain natural framework which pertains to reproduction, to one's own perception as a pregnant woman, is tied together by facts, by the fact of reproduction as characteristic of human beings, by the perception of one's body, by the social meaning of pregnancy, by attitudes, gestures, and language. This is already the form thought takes in these circumstances, and that, however, we can also picture as thought *about* these circumstances and which we can distinguish from them all the more in light of the reflective distance we can establish from them.

The picture of the relation between thought and frameworks I am presenting is the one we find at work in Wittgenstein's philosophy. For example, in the opening sections of the *Philosophical Investigations*, Wittgenstein asks in what naming an object consists, and imagines various scenes in which we can recognize this linguistic activity, in which we call an object by its name.[3] This linguistic activity is nothing but what people in those circumstances do, it belongs entirely to those circumstances, and Wittgenstein's philosophical interest lies in freeing us from the impression that there would and should be something else, that such activity trades in some immaterial substance in which meaning and thought consist as if they would consist in something different from the simple web of activities in which it happens that someone tells someone else: "Bring me a slab." What we describe as the kind of intellectual activity that has to do with calling an object with its name does not belong to a different plane—the immaterial one of thought—but is simply a way of describing what goes on in those circumstances. However, to describe those circumstances means entering the world that weave them together, and, as we know, such a world is made of facts, relationships, attitudes, and so on. What I have been doing so far is to make this point in relation to the themes of human life. Highly sophisticated intellectual activities—unlike simply calling something with its name, a slab, for example—such as those of reflecting on the goods and evils or on what is right and wrong at the beginning and at the end of life and in the field of sexuality—might be pictured as movements that belong to frameworks, to specific places determined by the intertwining of multiple activities and circumstances, among which those defining what it means to be born, die, and love. As a consequence, in this perspective, the diverse forms that moral thinking can take might be described by reference to the different frameworks where it finds its place, e.g. to different concepts of birth, death, and sexuality.

Let me remark once again the two aspects belonging to the very notion of a background: shaping thought but also letting it free to progress in unexpected directions. On the one hand, the framework is something objective, as it shapes and configures the form of our experience and ways of thinking. In this respect, Stanley Cavell writes, quite effectively, that "you cannot make words mean what you wish (*by* wishing)."[4] The free movement of our linguistic life—and this holds for the life of our experience and encounters with reality across the board—is determined by our linguistic, emotional, cognitive, and still other resources, resources which shape the world in which we live with different degrees of freedom depending on the nature of such a world and the kind of people we are. As we have seen, we may consider rather different moral orientations, for example, the conservative and the liberal ones in light of these backgrounds. In a world such as that of democratic societies, which has treasured the acquisitions I mentioned and is also the precipitate of older and long-lasting traditions, stances such as those of the conservatives and the liberals establish rather complex relationships with the framework in which they are set. I have claimed that what characterizes them is indeed a form of concealment and a disguise of this very relationship.

The second feature should be equally stressed. It regards the relationship of each of us, or better of the self, with this objective dimension that shapes our ways of experiencing and thinking. I have presented frameworks as human spaces, as the primary ways in which we experience life. They have an objective character, as we cannot change this reality at will and as we please. We move within spaces we have not created ourselves. But within the limits and in the modalities in which we move around in these spaces, through our experience and thought, we do extend or transform or contribute to unsettle or dismantle such frameworks. They are out there and objective, and yet they depend in each moment on one's personal contribution. The concept of reproduction as a particular kind of process characterized by attitudes, sentiments, and relationships, depends on vast biological, technological, and cultural facts, but it is that kind of concept because it pertains to the ways of living life in that area, of experiencing it and reflecting on it: activities that are performed by individual pregnant women (and also by all of us), and over which each woman casts her own spell—which in turn depends both on the nature of the framework itself and on her own personal situation—, marking one's contribution and making something personal out of such experience and thought.

We can then account for the nature of frameworks as the core of activities, attitudes, and relationships entangled with facts and that generate areas of experience and thought. But we can also account for their nature from the point of view of the self, of the ways in which our experience and thought, on the one hand, depend on objective fields, such as, for example, on what the body communicates to us, transmits to us, and allows us to feel, and on the power of words to mean, which are already there and in which we are situated; on the other hand, these objective fields have this power because we do confer it on them in the first place. The power of the various fields—such as those of the body and language—to speak to us with experiences and meanings depends on us, on our belonging to them—something to which we can, in certain circumstances, offer our contribution or refuse to do so. We can consider the diverse ethical orientations in this perspective as well, that is, with respect to how they acknowledge or rather conceal the relationship that frameworks establish with our self.

4.2 An elitist conservatism? What do conservatives learn from the notion of a background

I have presented the notion of a background as a way of reinterpreting the history of our moral culture and of securing new tools with which to defend what we care about and resist what we oppose—in particular, to guard the liberal and democratic achievements of the past and to further the struggles for freedom and subjectivity. I would now like to discuss what it means to think and defend one's moral commitments and goals in light of this notion. What does this reinterpretation of ourselves and history offer us? First of all, it helps to clarify and deepens our critical consciousness of our own situation, making us more aware and reflective with respect to our attachment to the positions and things we care about. In this light, my idea can be sensibly placed in the long tradition that begins with Socrates and claims that the examined life, that is, the life on which we cast our critical reflection, is better than the life shielded from critical consciousness. But this approach offers an important contribution to the two main contenders of modern moral culture.

It offers it to the conservatives, who, first of all, learn from it the difficulty of activating the full scope of the framework which breathes life into their judgments. They learn not only the difficulties related to the setting of the teleological machinery in motion as such but also acknowledge that the latter really is but a signpost, so to speak, of much broader and more articulated conceptual spaces, and hence they need to check the limits within which it is possible to activate them and what space they leave to other frameworks and concepts, among which those of freedom, interests, and subjectivity that are so crucial in modern societies. In this new perspective, the conservatives face a dilemma: either they reject the modern world in its entirety as a place that leaves no space for their concepts and ideals, or they rethink their concepts and ideals as personal possibilities that do not ignore or dismiss the scene dominated by the concepts of freedom and subjectivity. Anscombe, as we have seen, took the first path. The second one is open as well, but only suits a certain kind of conservative thinker. They are both hard calls, ones which indeed go against the grain: usually, contemporary conservatives refuse to take either the first or second paths and deny that there are conflicts of this kind between their stances and modern life.

I would like to pause for a moment on the second path, taken by those conservative thinkers who find in the modern world the conditions to rethink their values. An example is the one offered by the tradition expressed in the past century by a line that runs from Simone Weil to Czesław Miłosz, for example.[5] The discovery, in these authors, of the importance of the hardness of reality, which has an order of its own independently of us, as against the softness of the self and of its desires, endorsed, according to them, by modern freedom, turns out to be the discovery of moral possibilities that make sense as forms of resistance to crucial streams of the modern world and which as a consequence take the modern world and its form for granted. Miłosz is particularly helpful to single out a much longer tradition of thinking—which lists among its heroes ambivalent authors such as Fyodor Dostoevsky, who was also engaged in defending the restoration, in Russia, of a Christian world alternative to that one of modern Enlightenment—in which we can include authors which Miłosz does not include, such as Wittgenstein, for whom it is precisely because the modern world has won, that science has won as the most credited intellectual enterprise to investigate nature and access truth, that one can mark a negative contrast with what matters most. Miłosz goes back many times to a line by Dostoevsky (from 1854) that reads: "if someone proved to me that Christ is outside the truth and that *in reality* the truth were outside of Christ, then I should prefer to remain with Christ rather than with the truth."[6] The fact that truth is unfolded by modern science allows to defend a different set of values, which are revealed precisely by the fact that they are excluded from what is true, values illuminated by this radical contrast with science.

Now, it is my claim that Wittgenstein's *Tractatus* sits rather well with this line. The kind of value held dear by Wittgenstein, the way in which he handles life, death, and such actions as suicide can be comprehended and defended only by marking a radical contrast with the linguistic and knowledge dimensions that are utterly unable to reach such a value, an important example of which is the scientific understanding of the world.[7] In the perspective of these conservatives—in which I list Wittgenstein for one aspect of his criticism—the elaboration of the space of values originates in one having accepted the framework of modern life and having established a radical contrast with it. We don't find in these authors the sort of nostalgic attitude that takes center stage in MacIntyre who longs for a lost world, but rather the acceptance of the actual world.[8] The reflective and moral work, in this case, is a personal one, even if it can have practical and concrete effects. In an author such as Miłosz, the subscription to conservative values takes the form of the stylization of his life through contrasts and oppositions of the kind I have been suggesting, which do not, by the way, deprive him of the possibility of enjoying the wealth of goods produced by the modern world and of which he availed himself, such as the good of democracy, which he enjoyed as an expatriate of communist dictatorship, the goods of science, medicine, freedom, and the Western comforts of San Francisco Bay.

These forms of conservatism could be taken as concessions to aestheticism. But the accusation of aestheticism can be redirected to those who care for appearances only, to the appearance of values one believes in, while in the cases at hand what could appear as aestheticism is instead the acknowledgment that adhering to these values can be only personal in character or for a few. The moral life sometimes allows for this seemingly aestheticist way of being practiced and lived. In this case, the form taken by the loyalty to conservative values shows the character of the conservative belief in a world that leaves no space for it. However, as I have been claiming and will be claiming with the help of Mill, subscribing to whatever cluster of values calls for personal investment, it has a deep and thoroughly personal aspect that cannot by any means be left to a simple appeal to the collective form of life. As a consequence, it is not only the conservatives—who have the modern world against them, so to speak—who need to be burdened with the weight of their convictions: this burden is on us all, including those liberals whom, in their own way, have the world on their side.

4.3 Crumbling reality: What liberals can learn – Part I

If the very idea of a background, in the approach I am outlining, might offer its contribution to the defense of conservative values, it appears particularly congenial to liberal positions. So far, I have been describing a very influential type of liberal in contemporary thought: those who reject this kind of unmasking and redescription of their own positions, refusing to let—in Bernard Williams's words—their moralism go. But there are other authors who criticize the conservative positions by taking a path that is very much akin to the one I am exploring. One such author is Richard Rorty.[9] His positions are quite elaborate, but one of his signature theses is that democracy can flourish only if it frees itself of the metaphysical task of finding foundations for the beliefs and theories that it professes, and hence if it emancipates itself from the very idea of there being a reality out there grounding one's commitments. The public, democratic, space should be dominated by the commitment to fight cruelty and suffering. We need instruments to detect the pain of others, which for Rorty consists of the various forms of literature that help us to sympathize with the suffering and humiliation of our fellow beings. We do not need to find a ground for democratic convictions, nor should we should engage in resisting foundations either, as that is a task internal to metaphysical thinking itself: we should, rather, resolutely abandon the mind-frame in which it mattered to hold that something is grounded in the first place, that *this* is true, that *this* is reality. It is precisely the plurality of perspectives on reality, the plurality of vocabularies that tell us about various kinds of reality, none of which is more grounded than the others, that deprives us of the instruments to oppress people in the name of a given description bestowed upon them. In conclusion, we do not need reality but are, rather, in need of the uncontrolled unpredictability of the power of redescription that deprive those willing to humiliate us of the "correct description" that allows them to disqualify and oppress us.

In my perspective, the idea of the crumbling of reality is at the same time important and troublesome. As I said, the idea of bringing areas of life such as reproduction, sexuality, and death under the concept of background leads these realities into a dimension that is woven together by human intervention: it brings them into the mobility and historicity of these backgrounds, into the mobility of experience and thought, it brings them in the scene portraying the possibility of individual contribution. For example, to understand the reality of birth as a background transforms the hardness of this reality into something possible, something which has to do with the range of human possibilities, of possible ways of organizing human life. But what is possible might also have been otherwise; to see it as possible, in this humanly rich sense of possibility, means being able to imagine alternative configurations. This idea is crucial to Wittgenstein and to Foucault alike. Foucault writes in this respect that:

> the work of the intellectual…is fruitful in a certain way to describe that which is, while making it appear as something that might not be, or that might not be as it is. Which is why this designation or description of the real never has a prescriptive value of the kind, "because this is, that will be." It is also why, in my opinion, recourse to history…is meaningful to the extent that history serves to show how that which is has not always been; that is, the things which seem most evident to us are always formed in the confluence of encounters and chances, during the course of a precarious and fragile history. What reason perceives as *its* necessity or, rather, what different forms of rationality offer as their necessary being, can perfectly well be shown to have a history; and the network of contingencies from which it emerges can be traced. Which is not to say, however, that these forms of rationality were irrational; it means that they reside on

a base of human practice and human history—and that since these things have been made, they can be unmade, as long as we know how it was that they were made.[10]

On a number of occasions, Foucault highlights the importance of tracing and reconstructing the lines of historical evolution that took place and which generated backgrounds and conceptual dimensions. For example, in *Abnormal*,[11] he unfolds the meeting point of various reconstructive lines having to do with rather different things, including: the history of how Christianity has created the body as the object of attention from the conscience and techniques of inspection such as confession; the history of what is monstrous and outside nature and normality; the history of the techniques of punishment and juridical systems; and the history of psychiatry and hence also the peculiar history of the connection of these two institutions, the juridical and the medical-psychiatric. He weaves these various histories together in order to reconstruct the cultural scene of late-nineteenth-century Europe—a scene still very much relevant for us today—which revolves around the notion of normality, and hence around the concern to signal what is abnormal and bring it back it to the norm. In so doing, Foucault shows how it is possible, that is, humanly possible—in a process that brings together facts, relations, attitudes, "the core of human practice and human history"—for there to be realities such as those represented by the "criminals," the "homosexuals," or the "perverts." These realities are brought into the space of freedom. We see them surfacing in the confluence of the histories he recounts. This operation allows for a number of key ethical moves, which have already appeared in my discussion. I shall mention two. In the first place, it allows for acknowledging how this reality shapes the space of our possible experiences—the way in which we face reality and reflect on it. We realize how this reality belongs to us and represents us and we grasp its unavoidable character. In the second place, bringing it within the range of the core of human practices and human history makes it possible to imagine how to transform it, how to impress changes on it, making it something on which we can actively intervene. As a consequence, the crumbling of reality—that is, the fact that reality is led back to the range of practical and historical possibilities—allows us to rethink it and hence to undermine all things cruel and oppressive we do in its name.

I would like to mention an even more specific example Foucault develops in his course on *Psychiatric Power*.[12] The entire volume emphasizes the birth of psychiatry in the nineteenth century as a way of dictating and strengthening reality, which is only externally reinforced by medicine, thus conferring a suitable scientific status on its practices. Foucault's thesis is that psychiatry's task was that of imposing the reality of the asylum and, by means of it, the reality of the society outside of it, so to overcome the recalcitrant will of the patient, of the fool, who was seen as someone refusing to consent to the demands of society, and, as a consequence, its goal was not that of treating patients according to the methods accumulated by medicine at that time. Psychiatry imposes the reality of the asymmetry of power, of the noble and the low; the reality of the linguistic codes with which doctors and the entire hierarchy identify themselves; it imposes the reality of needs, hunger, hygiene, clothing, and money, and hence invests it with value; the reality of oneself, of one's history and identity, of where one was born, what one has done, and so forth; the reality of the external world as opposed to one's intimate pleasures, working on the force possessed by external reality to thwart the capacity of pleasures to adapt and bloom even in the most severe conditions. Foucault articulates these various maneuvers through which reality is reinforced, showing how things such as the need for money, being thirsty, needing clean clothes, using certain expressions rather than others, or knowing certain things about oneself, get transformed into a hard and unassailable reality, into something that resists delirium.

In this way, Foucault unmasks a technique of dictating reality that is at work in other spheres as well, and which matters to us all. He shows how reality is constituted, for each of us, as something hard that binds our movements and that we can smash into; at the same time, this description gives us the instruments to think of the hardness of reality as something made of facts for sure (biting hunger, the need to cover oneself, and so forth), but also of human activities, of relationships between people, of power relations between individuals and bodies, of all the sum of aspects that I have been collecting under the label of a framework. But if it is a human scene that we recognize, it is then a scene upon which we can impress turns and changes. In the years in which he was working on the materials I have discussed, Foucault only saw these movements in negative terms, that is, as forms of resistance, which seemed to lack full creative, subjective, and first-person force—a possibility he would highlight only later on in the 1980s, following a change in descriptive strategy. However, my aim was to underline this line that I have borrowed from Foucault and which is influential for an author such as Rorty: namely, the idea that the crumbling of the hardness of reality has an ethical quality to it, as it allows us to free ourselves of the supports onto which the oppressors secure their views.

4.4 The importance of reality: What liberals can learn – Part 2

There is another side to things to which the idea of the crumbling of reality is blind to, and which should be emphasized. I have touched on this further side already. As a matter of fact, these positions repeat a modality of critique that we encountered during the examination of the clash between liberals and conservatives. The positions insisting on the crumbling of reality criticize the metaphysical stances that turn the idea of *reality* into a way of imposing their own particular conceptions, and are led this way to the criticism of all possible notions of reality. This appears to be Rorty's view, which holds that liberals are equally equipped with their own metaphysics, offering a ground justifying their own positions, and encourages us to abandon the very concept of metaphysics altogether, and with it those of foundation and reality.

We have every reason to find this move unsatisfying and refuse to go from the criticism of the metaphysical conceptions of reality to the criticism of the notion of reality as such. We can agree with Rorty that the liberals have their own metaphysics: the criticism of liberalism as a form of moralism—which I have borrowed from Williams—is a relative of the criticism of the concept of metaphysics. Williams in effect criticizes what, to the liberals, look like ahistorical and a priori foundations, and claim that they inhabit the very same level of the theories for which they aim to offer foundations: in this sense, he unmasks the alleged metaphysical grounding of their theories. In its own way, the criticism raised by Sen to the theories which he brings under the concept of transcendental institutionalism goes in the same direction. He unmasks what look like the a priori foundations of ethical and political reflection—characteristic in particular of the various forms of contractualism—and redescribes them as participants in an open discussion among equals. However, positions such as those of Williams and Sen are not willing to do without the possibility of distinguishing between arguments that can be defended convincingly and those that cannot: that is, between grounded and ungrounded arguments. They do not want to get rid of the notions of ground and reality: they criticize the moves which locate grounds and reality beyond the reach of those very beliefs calling for them and bring them back at the level of the beliefs and convictions that ask for grounds. In the hands of these authors, what needs to be unmasked is the move that shifts reality and the grounds of what we believe and profess in an unreachable place and not the very appeal to grounds and reality as such.

The extension of the notion of metaphysics to any reflective exercise on the sources of one's understanding of things and one's practical commitments is, then, unconvincing. What I am defending, in general terms, is actually Wittgenstein's view. Wittgenstein, in the reading I defend, hinges his philosophical work on the very possibility of distinguishing between a metaphysical conception of reality—which hides the move through which such a conception fastens the possible movement of thought to reality—and an elucidation of the reality fastened to our human activities, disclosing its relationship with thought. Metaphysics, in Wittgenstein, far from signaling any form of appeal to what offers reasons in favor of the things we believe, rather indicates the unacknowledged modalities through which thought is fastened to reality and which take the form of mythologies. Rorty makes any appeal to reality and justification a form of mythology, while, for and with Wittgenstein, we can make distinctions. These are the kind of distinctions we find in authors such as Williams and Sen.

This is the position I have been defending. It is crucial to acknowledge the reality of frameworks: from the internal point of view, from which we realize that areas of human life are shaped by frameworks providing the setting for our experience and thought, frameworks are indeed real. An idea of reality that would keep its distinctive hardness is simply fundamental if we do not want to lose the notion of framework itself. Once again, Cavell's point about the impossibility of meaning something simply by willing it proves to be relevant: what we can mean depends on linguistic resources, on an entire world shaping our possibilities of linguistic movement, which it is not in our power to achieve by a simple act of will. Analogously, we cannot have a certain experience by simply willing it: to feel something presupposes forms of experience in which we are immersed, a world of experience, realities such as those which define the power of the body to produce sensations, pleasures, and meanings. We cannot give up the idea of the hardness of reality if we don't want to lose this entire landscape of aspects. Rorty insists on the pluralism of vocabularies, which translates into the pluralism of realities to which we have access. But if we want to account for the experience of meaning something, for the power of words to convey meanings, and for the experience of feeling certain kinds of pleasures, we should make room for a hard matter that cannot be created or modified at will, a matter granted with the power to account for the reality of meaning and pleasure, among other things. If we do not want to condemn these things to irrelevancy, to make them thin and superficial, if we want to weave an entire world around them—a world we can inhabit, to use Iris

Murdoch's expression[13]—then we should account for them in their hard and ramified reality, a reality which is independent of our sheer will, a reality which—once again with Murdoch[14]—it makes sense to discover and deepen: a reality so thick and complicated that it makes sense to find our place and position in it, or else to resist it as utterly oppressive and appalling. What makes so deep the relationship with one's language, with one's texture of experience, with the body and with the pleasures and meanings it is able to produce, the relationship with others and with their existence, and with the natural world—what makes all this so humanly deep is that it responds to the indefinite, vast, and articulate reality of language, of the body, of people, and of the natural environment.

The hardness of reality is, then, important in accounting for our human world of experiences. But this notion of reality is also important for the moral goals I have been defending, namely, for the struggles for freedom and subjectivity. In the achievements of the past, which need to be rethought and re-lived (or realized), and in current struggles, what we claim are *realities*: we claim the fact of being women, being gay and lesbian, being sick, being old, or being something different which resist these descriptions. At any rate, we claim states of being that are also those concrete and hard realities on which we are able to ground the interests we claim, our subjectivity, and our freedom. The freedom and the interests we claim do not derive from the abolition of reality but are rather grounded in the reality we experience. This reality can be something easily gained, something that is part of the world we have secured or can rather be a reality which lives in contrast with the existing reality, in the resistance to it or in the little independent spaces one has been able to carve out of it. But it is reality nonetheless. As a consequence, from the point of view of the defense of the democratic achievements and of the new struggles for subjectivity, we should not dismiss the idea according to which there is something like human life, but rather interrogate which kinds of human life make specific forms of freedom possible. We rely on thought, imagination, and on the visible traces in the present of a desirable future; we recruit all we can to gather enough reality about ourselves, about our desires and our pleasures to be claimed and woven together with the experience of other people in order to give form to new ways of living.

When Foucault examined the Scottish eighteenth-century tradition—which as I have said represents one of the lines akin to the one I am defending—he offered some quite useful considerations.[15] He saw how in that tradition there was the discovery of the hard and unassailable reality of what we feel, of our desires, which function as a resistance to oppression. In the context of the forms of power characteristic of absolutist states, which shape the population from above as a source of wealth, military power, and influence on the international stage, Foucault rediscovers in a tradition of economists and philosophers—from Hume to Smith to Ferguson—an appeal to desire as the key moment of a broader attack on an artificialist conception of the sovereign, of a defense of civil society and with it of a form of government which limits itself in the face of a material—population, wealth, life, and so on— which it has the power neither to create at will nor to exhaustively know and, hence, nor to control entirely. Individual desire emerges here as an element of resistance against absolutist power and is part of the defense of the freedom of individuals. Foucault speaks of a desire "one can do nothing against."[16] The statement he finds in Hume, according to which at the end of every practical reasoning there would be a desire of some sort,[17] is read as the defense of an individuality that cannot be further traversed by the sovereign power, the individuality of a "subject of individual choices which are both irreducible and non-transferable." He writes that "what is important is the appearance of interest for the first time as a form of both immediately and absolutely subjective will."[18]

Desires here appear to Foucault in the way I think they should be defended: not as forms of negations of reality, but rather as the expression of the reality of one's subjectivity, a hard reality which is able to resist the power which aims at shaping bodies and minds from its point of view. The moral considerations and struggles in the areas of human life considered have exactly this form. They are struggles to claim the reality of one's experience of the pregnant body, of one's sexual desire and pleasures, of one's sensations and thoughts about death. Through the defense of, and struggle for, freedom and subjectivity, we elaborate and articulate the dimension to which our desires give voice, and oppose it, in its reality and unavoidability, to the alternative intellectual configurations that do not see it, that deny it and oppress it. For these reasons, as I have tried to argue, if we lose sight of reality, we lose sight of the ground for the defense of freedom and subjectivity with it.

Notes

1 Both aspects have been treated by two authors who are crucial to my perspective: namely, Stanley Cavell and Cora Diamond. See Cavell, *The Claim of Reason*, op. cit.; Diamond, "Losing Your Concepts," op. cit., p. 268: "Learning to use a term is coming into life with that term, whose possibilities are to a

great extent to be made." See also Diamond, "Unfolding Truth and Reading Wittgenstein." *Sats: Nordic Journal of Philosophy*, 4, 2003, pp. 24–58. Also, see the way in which John McDowell puts together the notion of the space of reasons with that of tradition in *Mind and World*, op. cit., Lecture V; also, McDowell, "Gadamer and Davidson on Understanding and Relativism," in *The Engaged Intellect. Philosophical Essays*, Cambridge (MA): Harvard University Press, 2009, pp. 134–151.

2 Alasdair MacIntyre, *After Virtue*, op. cit., pp. 52–53.

3 Ludwig Wittgenstein, *Philosophische Untersuchungen. Philosophical Investigations* (1953), ed. by G.E.M. Anscombe and R. Rhees, Oxford: Blackwell, 1967. See the interpretation offered by Stanley Cavell in his "Notes and Afterthoughts on the Opening of Wittgenstein's Investigations," in *Philosophical Passages: Wittgenstein, Emerson, Austin, Derrida*, Oxford: Blackwell, 1995, pp. 125–186.

4 Stanley Cavell, "Must We Mean What We Say?" in *Must We Mean What We Say? A Book of Essays* (1969), Cambridge: Cambridge University Press, 1976, p. 39.

5 Czesław Miłosz, *The Land of Ulro*, New York: Farrar, Straus & Giroux, 1981. See also Miłosz, *Emperor of the Earth. Modes of Eccentric Vision*, Berkeley: University of California Press, 1977.

6 Fyodor Dostoevskij, *Complete Letters. Vol. 5: 1868–1871*, ed. by David A. Lowe, Ann Arbor: Ardis, p. 142; Czesław Miłosz, *The Land of Ulro*, op. cit., p. 266.

7 Ludwig Wittgenstein, *Tractatus logico-philosophicus*, with an English translation by C.K. Ogden, London: Routledge & Kegan Paul, 1922. On this interpretation, see Cora Diamond, "Ethics, Imagination, and the Method of Wittgenstein's Tractatus" (1991), in *The New Wittgenstein*, ed. by A. Crary and R. Read, London: Routledge, 2000, pp. 149–173; James Conant, "The Method of the Tractatus", in *From Frege to Wittgenstein: Perspectives on Early Analytic Philosophy*, ed. by E. Reck, Oxford: Oxford University Press, 2002, pp. 374–462. See also Piergiorgio Donatelli, "The Problem of 'The Higher' in Wittgenstein's Tractatus," in *Religion and Wittgenstein's Legacy*, ed. by D.Z. Phillips and M. von der Ruhr, Aldershot: Ashgate, 2005, pp. 11–38.

8 Alasdair MacIntyre, *After Virtue*, op. cit., Chapter 18.

9 See in particular Richard Rorty, *Contingency, Irony and Solidarity*, Cambridge: Cambridge University Press, 1989. See also the discussion by James Conant, "Freedom, Cruelty, and Truth: Rorty versus Orwell," in *Rorty and His Critics*, ed. by R.B. Brandom, Oxford: Blackwell, 2000, pp. 268–342.

10 Michel Foucault, "Structuralism and Post-Structuralism," in *Essential Works of Michel Foucault 1954–1984. Vol. 2: Aesthetics, Method, and Epistemology*, ed. by James D. Faubion, New York: The New Press, 1998, p. 450.

11 Michel Foucault, *Abnormal*, op. cit.

12 Michel Foucault, *Psychiatric Power. Lectures at the Collège de France 1973–1974*, ed. by A.I. Davidson, New York: Palgrave Macmillan, 2006. See, in particular, the lesson of 19 December 1973.

13 Iris Murdoch, "On 'God' and 'Good'," in *Existentialists and Mystics*, op. cit., p. 337.

14 Iris Murdoch, "The Idea of Perfection," op. cit.

15 Michel Foucault, *Security, Territory, and Population. Lectures at the Collège de France 1977–1978*, ed. by A.I. Davidson, London: Palgrave Macmillan, 2007; *The Birth of Biopolitics. Lectures at the Collège de France 1978–1979*, ed. by A.I. Davidson, London: Palgrave Macmillan, 2008.

16 Michel Foucault, *Security, Territory, and Population*, op. cit., p. 72.
17 David Hume, *An Enquiry Concerning the Principles of Morals*, ed. by T. Beauchamp, Oxford: Oxford University Press, 1998, p. 88: "It is impossible there can be a progress *in infinitum*; and that one thing can always be a reason, why another is desired. Something must be desirable on its own account, and because of its immediate accord or agreement with human sentiment or affection."
18 Michel Foucault, *The Birth of Biopolitics*, op. cit., pp. 272-273.

Chapter 5

The struggle for freedom

5.1 The opponents of freedom

5.1.1 Freedom and subjectification

I have listed two adversaries opposing the claim for freedom and subjectivity: the traditional picture—which ties teleology, social meanings, and the divine law together—and the picture treating science and technology as privileged modalities of access to reality. In Chapters 2 and 3, I began to show how these perspectives leave no space for the formation of specific ways of life promoting freedom and the nurturing of personal interests. In Chapter 2, I redescribed the clash between liberals and conservatives as a confrontation between frameworks, between overall visions of human life. Once the notion of a background is introduced, it is possible to acknowledge a further, previously invisible opponent of freedom, which hides behind the idea that freedom needs a notion of nature devoid of human meanings, to be handled by science and technology. In Chapter 3, we saw how science and technology take over natural processes for their own goals, which are not entirely our own unspecialized goals. In this chapter, I would like to elaborate on the framework of freedom that the liberals disown. Before doing that, I shall go back to the traditional framework and the scientific-technological one in order to verify how they are equally unfit to promote freedom and rather pursue different goals. I will say more on the former (§5.1.1) and be briefer on the latter (§5.1.2).

The first opponent is simply unfit to produce freedom. It works by subjecting (to use Foucault's language) individuals.[1] The picture of a heteronomous divine law empties the human scene of the materials that the self might rework in personal and creative ways and describes the movement of the self as having the sole task of acting in accordance with what God commands. There is a vivid picture offered by the biblical story of Isaac's sacrifice. We understand what it means, in the framework of the divine law—a framework that is real and alive in the biblical tale—to think of duty as coming from the will of God: it means emptying the human scene of all other meanings. In the parable, there are indeed many such meanings at work: the life of Isaac, that of Abraham and his relation to another human being, who happens to be his son, an entire world made up of human beings, with their existences, concerns, and relations, a rich human world that does not, however, contribute at all to understanding what our duty is. It seems to me that the point of the trial that God throws at Abraham—it is indeed a trial, as at the latest moment God stays Abraham's hand—is precisely to show that if God were to ask, we should be all obliged to do this as well, and this means that the source of duty is entirely exhausted by the divine law, and has nothing to do with the texture of human sentiments, relations, interests, and loyalties. Søren Kierkegaard, who reflected deeply on this extraordinary episode, did not want to compromise its absurd character, and used it specifically to disjoin ethics from religion: if religion truly regulated our lives, it would be incompatible with ethics, as it would annihilate it.[2] This observation by Kierkegaard is voiced at the end of the long dominion of the divine law conception when it seemed hardly possible to sincerely believe that the divine law could be the source of morals, and the only way out was to resolutely keep the two spheres apart. Let us not forget that this very move is a part of the general strategy at work in modernity: with the disintegration of the unitary medieval framework, the various spheres (religion, morality, law, science) separated and gained independence from one another. Kierkegaard's move is similar to Dostoevsky's, who separated Christ from the truth. In the modern world, according to these great Christian thinkers, both knowledge and morality now occupy a different area, in which these authors were unable to place the religious values dear to them. A dispassionate exam that does not evade the difficulties posed by modernity, such as Kierkegaard's, shows us the reality of divine law: the latter is incompatible with the free exercise of one's subjectivity but is rather aimed at shaping one's individuality in accordance with something that lies completely outside of oneself, and hence has a form that is *not* ethical, not in the way ethics has been gradually conceived in the centuries of modernity.

For a more detailed analysis, we should do better to follow Foucault once again and consider the specific ways in which divine law has been cashed out with the emergence of the Christian pastoral power in the first centuries of the new era, with multiple changes in the many subsequent centuries, punctuated by such crucial steps as those at the dawn of the new millennium and then the Counter-Reformation, starting from the

Council of Trent. What we would see, following Foucault's narration, is the invention—borrowing from doctrinal materials and techniques belonging to the Hebrew and oriental traditions but in particular to the philosophical schools of the late empire—of techniques for controlling souls in which it is utterly impossible to make room for the free exercise of one's subjectivity. These are techniques that seek to shape one's interiority in light of interests, of a search for the self, and of modalities of personal relations such as confession that issue into subjection, creating individuals motivated by an interest in scrutinizing themselves so as better to obey their pastor, individuals whose space of movement is that of subjecting themselves to the will of someone who in turn conveys the will of God and of God's law.[3]

The other axis along which the traditional framework is articulated is that of teleology. As with the previous case, there is no production of freedom but rather the shaping of a scene in which the exercise of one's faculties is directed to the conforming with the intrinsic order of reality. In the teleological picture, a sphere such as that of sexuality, for example, is seen as a place in which ends are displayed: we interrogate it by asking about its function. In the Christian picture, the answer is, obviously, procreation. As a consequence, virtue consists in conforming as well as possible to the proper end of this sphere of life. What we need to be doing as virtuous individuals in such an area is to exercise fully the function that defines such a domain. The passage from function to duties might be more complicated than this: Anscombe, for example, clarifies that there are a number of intermediate passages. Duties are directed to the intention that characterizes an action as that particular kind of conduct; the teleological context confers on a certain kind of action its very character it has, for example, the generative one. As a consequence, as individuals, we are required to respect those duties that command us to perform actions that exemplify the appropriate teleological character (e.g., its generative character). In this light, the prohibition to use birth control methods forbids a kind of conduct that, if performed, would prevent the sexual activity from being intrinsically generative, from having its teleologically appropriate character.[4] In this picture, teleology allows for an analogous move to the one carried out by means of the divine law: our duties are traced exclusively to what is appropriate to do conceived of as the exercise of the function that describes a certain area. The complex area of sexuality is then traced exclusively to the understanding of the end inscribed in it.

To follow this line of reasoning is no easy task. It is, in fact, congenial when staged against a theological background. In this case, the question about which end characterizes a specific sphere of life is related to the idea that there would be an author of nature who created it and acted intentionally, and that it would then be appropriate to ask why there is such reality in the first place: an answer that, departing from the description of an organism, goes back to the act that produced it and hence to the reasons for such an act. Similar considerations apply if we try the teleological picture with human artefacts about which it seems to be completely appropriate to ask why they are produced as they are. In such a case, the description of the artefact indicates its function and the latter points to the maker of the artefact. In the case of artefacts, it then makes sense to offer an account of the non-moral value of the object along these lines. Within the limits in which the clock's function is to tell the time—and does not have other uses, aesthetic ones and so on—, we go back from the function to the value of the object: the clock is a good clock proportionally to how it fulfills its function of telling the right time. But if we do not think of nature as created by someone by means of an intentional act, of which it thus makes sense to ask the reasons why she so acted, it is less clear what it would mean to apply the teleological picture to nature and to human beings in particular. In ancient cultures, teleology was part of a conception that did not disjoin the natural world from the human one, and as a consequence, it seemed appropriate to account for it in teleological terms. But in ancient culture as well, the role of teleology was probably not the one attributed to it by Christian culture and contemporary conservatism alike. John McDowell has argued, for example, that, in Aristotle, the appeal to *ergon* does not refer to a general teleology that would give ethical reasons for appropriate virtues all by itself. This appeal does nothing but establishing a truism between what is appropriate to do for human beings and what is excellent for them, while the very content of excellence is to be discovered from within the point of view of the virtuous person by means of instruments that involve rather different resources.[5]

Perhaps, then, it is not that easy to find in classical culture examples in which teleology is introduced as the very foundation of ethics. And yet my point is the following: even if we could understand what it means to ground ethics in a teleology built into organisms and their parts, this would clearly be a way of leaving the point of view of the individuals out of the picture. If we thought that human beings were created with their various faculties and capacities for determinate reasons, similarly to how the meat industry produces a certain brand of chicken in order to obtain breasts to wrap in cellophane for supermarkets, these reasons would not exhaust the practical understanding of these beings. Even if we were to describe human beings in such a way, they would still see things from their own point of view: even if we would describe them teleologically, this would not exhaust the space of experience in the first person, where they articulate reasons that are not those available by offering a description of those kinds of beings from without, but rather those springing from the experience in the first person. The teleological picture, thus, similarly to that of the divine law, does not admit the free exercise of subjectivity: it simply does not consider it.

Finally, the axis of the social meanings of the various spheres of nature belonging to the traditional picture is equally at odds with freedom, as we have seen. These concepts express attestations of respect toward life and are far from congenial to the first-person exercise of freedom. Let me recall, one more time, that neither in the traditional picture nor in the contemporary conservative positions do we find reference to any of these axes alone. Even when, for example, the reference to the divine law is set aside, the appeal to teleology and to the social meanings of actions, to modesty, honor, reverence or shame all work together to articulate an overall background.

5.1.2 Freedom and normalization

As we saw in Chapter 3, the other opponent of freedom and subjectivity is the one that presents science and technology as the sources of privileged access to areas of human life. The scientific-technological conception is not functional to the production of freedom, its aim is rather to lead its object to its own epistemic and practical goals. In particular, as Foucault has shown us, it normalizes life. Let us bear in mind that every description places its object under a certain concept, and hence it brings something contingent under a universal, exercising in this way the pressure of logical necessity onto some contingent aspects. If, for example, we call something love, such a concept transforms the things we feel, observe, tell, and so on, by bringing them together under the normative force of the concept of love. Therefore, the fact that scientific and technological descriptions are normative in character is not the point of the criticism. The point is rather the kind of normativity featuring them. They are not aimed at accounting for something and operating on it in response to unspecialized human needs, needs regarding the wide spectrum of human faculties—the primary human potentialities, as I have called them—, but rather in response to specialized aims and interests, cognitive and practical alike.

Furthermore, after Foucault, we are in a position to underline the collaboration between the two enterprises, epistemological and practical, that is, the ways in which specialized inquiries issue in kinds of knowledge that are in the service of practical ends. Medicine in all its various branches avails itself of different sorts of knowledge, but it is at the same time an epistemic endeavor aimed at the practical goal of treatment. Furthermore, the epistemic work involved in medicine is used outside of medical practice, for example, in courts, by legislators to plan social policies, and so on. In addition, specialization has the power to boost its own effects. Kinds of specialized knowledge have a dimension of their own that does not respond to non-specialized human interests, which at least in some branches of science can be explained as the inquiry into how things are out there, the dispassionate search for truth. This is a specialized interest and is not an interest in knowing the reality that is part of non-specialized human interests—for example, the reality of the beloved person as an internal goal tied to willing her good—, even if it is in our non-specialized human interest to secure this knowledge—or, better, to trust those who discover and disseminate it. In the case of technology, there is a boosting effect involved because the knowledge that touches reality with its specialized conceptual dimension has specialized practical goals, such as those of treatment, of minimizing risk, or obtaining results in terms of public policies.

These practical endeavors have a normalizing character. They offer descriptions and mobilize techniques aimed at issuing in normality, at making reality conform to the description of it given by a given specialized discipline: for example, in terms of health and disease, risk and uncertainty, and so on. The domain of normality is rather complex, but we can identify at least two varieties. The first is the normality that inscribes the idea of a norm and the deviation from the norm into nature, typical, for example, of nineteenth-century psychiatry and psychoanalysis. The second is the statistical normality of those social sciences with an economic basis.[6] In both cases, even if quite differently so, the individual is pictured, treated, and offered instruments to handle herself with knowledge and techniques that do not envisage the free exercise of her subjectivity, they do not have in view self-discovery and self-invention. The concept of sexuality as a crucial dimension of psychoanalysis introduces an idea of normality that does not include the possibility of living one's sexuality inventively, but rather requires one to conform to a norm, acknowledging, for example, one's desires and interests as cases falling under psychoanalytic descriptions—say, perversions. In a different way, the concept of sexuality as a dimension of statistical normality traces conducts back to a determinate description offered in statistical terms functional to public knowledge and policies, for example, in terms of risk, which are equally blind to the fact that those conducts give expression to one's subjectivity. Freedom needs to turn conducts and states of being into forms of subjectivity, as in a story told in the first person of the quest for happiness and of the ends shaping one's existence: not in psychological terms or in those of the social sciences. Freedom needs primary moral work, through which we encounter experience and learn from it in ways that are not seen from the unavoidably third-person point of view of specialized knowledge and its concepts.[7]

5.2 From dispositives to frameworks: John Stuart Mill

We have examined some significant opponents of freedom. We are now in a position to ask how a framework that is hospitable to freedom and the creative exercise of subjectivity should look like. In the perspective I have sketched, the advocates of liberalism themselves lack the necessary reflective resources to answer this question. The defense of the various dispositives, of the principles and institutions, that preserve freedom are not enough, but we need the entire framework to create individuals and relations. With Foucault, the liberation from oppression is crucial, yet hardly sufficient: what is needed is the realization of the very conditions in which we can take active care of freedom. As he wrote in an interview:

> When an individual or social group succeeds in blocking a field of power relations, immobilizing them and preventing any reversibility of movement by economic, political, or military means, one is faced with what may be called a state of domination. In such a state, it is certain that practices of freedom do not exist or exist only unilaterally or are extremely constrained and limited. Thus, I agree with you that liberation is sometimes the political or historical condition for a practice of freedom.

However, he continues, "liberation paves the way for new power relationships, which must be controlled by practices of freedom."[8]

Liberation from oppression tears down certain features of the vast fabric of aspects, relations, perceptions, attitudes, and activities constituting the basis of our being individuals; it tears down fundamental and crucial features, and yet it could leave the wider basis which facilitates the exercise of oppression unaltered. In this light, Foucault's criticism of the juridical model proves to be useful, including under this label not only the oppressors but also the various perspectives holding that we can free ourselves from the state of oppression by establishing new juridical and contractual forms, which, however, leave out of the picture the broader region of what the Scottish philosophers called civil society.[9] In order not to leave the broader basis unaltered, we need to secure a position from which this basis is fully in view, so as to be able, on the one hand, to think of moral reflection as the expression of this broader basis and, on the other—since it is an expression that takes the shape of experience and thought, and hence it is capable of distancing itself from it—, to critically examine it, to affect changes and transformations or nurture the need for its radical reformation. What is the distinctive form of a society where freedom and the interest in exercising one's subjectivity in creative, personal, and inventive ways bloom, seen from the point of view of this broader basis?

In order to give an answer, we must go back to Mill. Mill understood the problem exactly in these terms: what form a society holding freedom dear should take? A society in which freedom is not visible only at determinate moments, such as in the exercise of the law and in the fruition of freedom it guarantees, or in the circumscribed moments of choice and of the expression of one's ideas. Mill, of course, defends these key dispositives of freedom: he is a classical author of liberalism even in this traditional sense, but at the same time he explains what it means to defend these dispositives in a way that radically transforms classical liberalism. He harshly criticizes the contractualist variety of liberalism because of its narrow focus on juridical forms and brings into the picture the broader basis constituted by the entire range of human faculties and by how they shape reality. Mill thought that, in order to defend freedom and subjectivity, we should picture the specific forms of life that shape the social space and the constitution of individuals so far as to reach the various spheres of life, the ways in which we are relational beings, women who give birth, individuals endowed with specific and particular forms of experience.

Let me break his argument down. Mill clearly saw what I have called the primary moral work, the work through which individuals constitute themselves as subjects who freely and creatively exercize their faculties. This theme surfaces in an area of his thought that we might label as perfectionist, using the term in the light of Stanley Cavell's rich elaboration of this notion, where Mill discusses and illustrates what it means to exercise one's individual faculties.[10] As Mill writes at the end of his *System of Logic*, we can consider what makes people happy:

> both in the comparatively humble sense, of pleasure and freedom from pain, and in the higher meaning, of rendering life, not what

> it now is almost universally, puerile and insignificant—but such as human beings with highly developed faculties can care to have.[11]

Individual life is transformed by the work of self-cultivation and self-education. In *On Liberty*—in chapters 2 and 3 in particular—Mill gets to the details of this transformation. The lives of people, the beliefs they have, the pleasures they feel, and the preferences they form, are transformed by the work on the self. We should thus visualize the relationship that the self establishes with its beliefs, pleasures and conducts, and consider what this supplies us with: whether it is a relationship capable of activating the self, its freedom and its capacity to constitute itself as a subject, or if it rather wears it off, making the self a deposit of beliefs, experiences, and conducts to which it conforms and that it merely receives from without. We cannot consider individual experiences as given in a philosophically unproblematic way, we should rather interrogate them from the point of view of the relationship they establish with the human individual considered as a progressive being. Mill is working here on the issue of the transformative character of the self, of its mobility, as a crucial question of freedom, which, as we have seen (Chapter 3, §3.4), is also the perspective defended by Foucault.

This is the wider context in which Mill situates his defense of the liberal society. He wishes to defend the conditions in which people are encouraged to consider themselves in the light of the relationship the self establishes with its contents, in the light of how the self educates and transforms itself or rather is subjected, in a state of conformity. Now, what are these conditions? Here we can find an answer to the requirements that surfaced in my criticism both of the traditional picture and of contemporary liberals. On the one hand, we need to defend freedom within the limits of the law and the institutions that guarantee it. Also, we need to defend the promotion of interests at least in the form of the defense of the quality of life and of social well-being. That is, we should defend the liberation from ancien régime society, grounded in illiberal and oppressive juridical systems and on a structural disinterest in the quality of life—if not in the active promotion of cruelty. Still, this is hardly sufficient: in Mill's view, these transitions are already behind us, they are possessions of modern civilized societies.[12] The problem we face, once the fight against traditional regimes has been won, is that of verifying how the spaces of freedom guaranteed by the law, institutions, and the totality of obligations characteristic of civilized societies get transferred into individual liberty, into the capacity and motivation to make something of oneself as a subject. Analogously, the question is also that of not considering personal experiences, pleasures and pains, as non-problematic data only, but rather to glimpse in them the expression of a subject who has made something of herself, to consider them as experiences that describe the inner texture of *her* character. In Mill's terms, it means relating the exercise of freedom as well as the promotion of interests to the conception of the individual as a progressive being. He, in fact, rethinks both utilitarianism and liberalism in these terms, reinterpreting them in the light of what I have called a perfectionist conception of the human individual.[13] He rethinks utility in terms of the experiences—and pleasures in particular—that are appreciated only by individuals who engage in a work on themselves, and rethinks the liberal warranties as modalities through which people are put in the condition to work on themselves, living in a state of constant attention to their own transformability.

In order to give an answer to the demands of freedom, Mill then thinks that we cannot be satisfied with the classical move of liberalism. As we know, such a move consists of the simple shift to another level: namely, that of the protection of liberal warranties and the promotion of interests. By leading the battle from that angle, the traditional picture is defeated only partially and locally: it is defeated when, for example, it promotes and actually glorifies the cruelty of punishment, or when it denies such fundamental liberties as those of free expression and association. Yet the comprehensive visions animating the traditional picture are not interrogated and are rather relocated from the heart of juridical power to the private space of individual conscience. Rather than considering these visions as the very pillars of the public space, once society is based on different grounds—those of freedom and the promotion of the quality of life—they are left exercising their influence in the form of convictions, ideas, and rules of conduct people nurture and follow in their individual lives. The mere relocation of traditional conceptions from the space shaping the public and constitutional architecture of society to the private space of conscience is but a different way of describing the liberal move on which I have commented and that I have criticized in the previous chapters. Now, this is the move criticized by Mill as well. If we are keen to consider autonomy and interests as possibilities of the self, if we want to picture them from the point of view of the relationship the self establishes with itself, then we should look at what shapes the self, at the modalities in which it entertains beliefs, experiments with pleasures, and tries conducts out. We should enter these areas and examine the mass of aspects shaping individual life, the wide bases of human response, and the frameworks to which they give life.

This is in effect the work in which Mill engages. He does not limit himself to shifting the philosophical explanation from the level of traditional frameworks to that of freedom and interests. In his terms, he is not only engaged in the defense of liberalism and utilitarianism, but also in rethinking them in light of the needs I have indicated, and which can be summed up around the concept of the individual as a progressive being, as a being who opens herself to the possibilities of transformation. The ground Mill covers is then that of criticizing the traditional picture, along the three dimensions I have mentioned, and of pointing to alternative possibilities, to outlining alternative frameworks of human life in which freedom is left blooming.

5.3 Mill on religion, family, and nature

Mill's goal is to examine and revise the materials shaping what he calls the "internal culture of the individual."[14] A liberal society needs individuals taking care of their internal culture, of the bases that shape their faculties and the use they make of them. In this light, he rethinks the various features of the traditional framework discussed previously such as religion, intimate and family relations, or the role of nature. These are examples of the kind of contrast around which I have built the present book. In the conservative understanding, these elements are weaved together in a homogeneous framework that does not work by producing freedom but rather conformity. In the liberal conception, they belong, on the one hand, to the discretionary personal sphere on which liberal universal principles have nothing to say in particular and, on the other hand, they count as interests that are part of the general interest of society. Mill is, rather, interested in criticizing these manners of existence to verify if they effectively result in freedom or if, rather, if they issue in states of being and forms of relations and social life that are out of tune with freedom.

Let us consider his position on religion: it is a liberal view indeed, grounded on the relocation of religious beliefs to the private sphere. However, this is no simple shift, but rather an overall revision of what religion means in the first place. According to Mill, only a certain kind of religion can count as a meaningful feature of the self, and grounds as such its inclusion under the principle of freedom. Mill, in particular, highlights the obstacle Christianity represented to the development of a public space shaped on the receptivity to the experience and the opinions of other people, even if he acknowledges the role played by the Church in the Middle Ages. To this end, his judgment is largely coherent with the picture I have been sketching. He claims that Catholicism played a notable civilizing role for many centuries during the Middle Ages; the Reformation played a crucial role during early modernity; but, after that, he grants no further positive role to confessional Christianity and more generally to religion, if not on the condition of its radical revision.[15] Religion represents an obstacle to the formation of a public morality based on discussion, on the revisability of opinions, on the repudiation of the sources of judgment preserved from criticism, equally impeding in this way the critical and reflective development of the self. Under the influence of religion, prevailing opinions are left unchecked and without criticism, while

> a large portion of the most active and inquiring intellects find it advisable to keep the general principles and grounds of their convictions within their own breasts, and attempt, in what they address to the public, to fit as much as they can of their own conclusions to premises which they have internally renounced.

A condition whose price is "the sacrifice of the entire moral courage of the human mind."[16] The Christian religion is "essentially a doctrine of passive obedience; it inculcates submission to all authorities found established":[17] there simply is no space for the active education of the sentiments and the constitution of the self as subject.

Mill, thus, is not satisfied with the defense of the principle of freedom, which guarantees the liberty to access religious confessions and make them one's guide in life. He asks if such conceptions and a society shaped by them allow for the exercise of freedom, if they indeed articulate a framework hospitable to freedom and subjectivity. In this light, he claims that Christian confessions, as he saw them at work in his society, are foes to freedom, even once the liberal guarantees defending the freedom of religious belief and personal convictions have been secured. There is still work to be done, which consists of transforming the overall frameworks of society in the light of the personal quest for freedom and happiness. Thus, Mill, on the one hand, refuses to stop short with regulatory achievements in the law and in moral principles—the protection of the freedom to express of one's convictions—and criticizes religions accordingly; on the other hand, he does not go along the Enlightenment mode of criticism which simply tries to get rid of the traditional theological picture, and rather questions which specific alternative forms of self-exercise allow for the cultivation of free subjectivities. Mill partly endorsed the nineteenth-century idea of translating Christianity into a civil religion on the Comtian model of the religion of humanity; furthermore, he was an atheist himself, despite the doubts expressed in his essay *Theism*.[18] His view though is not that of a simple replacement of confessional religion with a civil atheistic one. His idea is that religion pertains to the most intimate spheres of the self; it is a dimension to which he ties the very possibility of elevation, development, and achievement of the self, the possibility of bestowing meaning on one's existence. These themes run through his entire intellectual biography, from the 1830s up to his last writings, to *The Utility of Religion* and the *Inaugural Address to the University of St. Andrews*.[19] For this reason, Mill did not share the skeptical idea of treating religion as sheer prejudice but rather aimed at rethinking some of its materials and techniques in order to see how they would be functional to the articulation of a way of believing and conducting oneself congenial to the constitution of the self as a free subject.

Another important example is that of family relationships. Mill engages in a complete, critical revision of the concept of family. He claims that it is not conceivable that the family can be considered as a territory foreign to civil and democratic society. I have covered the considerations advanced in *The Subjection of Women* already. What goes on in the household has tremendous consequences for the individuals involved and society in its entirety. A model of the family grounded on the division of roles and on male supremacy cannot but corrupt the morality of all of its members, of the man who learns an authoritarian and despotic attitude from it, of the woman who gets accustomed to a condition of subjection, and of the children who are raised in an environment that does not educate them to justice but rather to inequality and to the oppression of one sex over another. Reproduction itself is an issue that needs to be handled and governed with prudence and responsibility, which are the obvious rules in the other areas of life, and clearly cannot be left to nature: that is, to chance.[20] If personal relations, reproductive choices, and the education of the offspring are crucial moments for the constitution of society, it is unimaginable to subject such a sphere to rules and attitudes that are foreign to those governing the rest of society. If we want to defend a society dominated by respect, freedom, and responsibility, we should aim to make these very values the guiding lights of intimate relations in the family and the education of children. But this revision of intimate and family relationships is also essential for the defense of individuals themselves. The possibility of becoming individuals requires a critical revision of the models guiding personal life. It requires us to acknowledge how all the intimate relationships we entertain with others play a pivotal role in the constitution of our persona. In this field too, therefore, Mill's task is not only that of shifting the sphere of personal and family relationships under the legislation of the principle of freedom, but rather to prompt us to interrogate ourselves on the forms of relations most congenial to the ways of life marked by freedom and the search for one's subjectivity.

We can find this philosophical scheme equally applied in Mill's treatment of the appeal to nature.[21] As we know, nature had been customarily considered as a site in which to unveil divine ends and designs and gather the rules for individual conduct. Mill launches quite a harsh campaign against these ideas. What we can count as progress and civilization of humanity required precisely a modification of nature, its use for clearly human goals. Moral criteria do not operate within the space created by those that we may consider as the aims of nature, but rather within the space of human interests. The appeal to nature plays the role of consecrating traditional rules of conduct and moral conceptions, sealing them with the mark of what is inscribed in the immutable order of things. We have seen already how according to the traditional picture and in the conservative one, there is a collaboration among the various axes. In particular, I have highlighted how the teleological picture of nature works as a seal that strengthens the conceptions deriving from the other axes.

Even in this area, however, his criticism not only shows how the traditional framework proves inadequate in accounting for our moral ideas but also interrogates us on the framework which would make these ideas a place we can inhabit. Once freed of teleology, nature not only becomes itself the object studied by science but also enters the moral interests of the individuals engaged in self-cultivation, engaged in a work on themselves. Mill places this kind of interest within a specific sphere of human evaluation that he calls aesthetics, a dimension pertaining to the modalities in which we work on the imagination by shaping ideals of life with which we enter in a relationship of emulation, and in which he also includes his revised notion of religion. Nature, in its dimensions of beauty, allure and greatness, has the power to transform the self in this way. He writes:

> there are few capable of feeling the sublimer order of natural beauty [...], who are not, at least temporarily, raised by it above the littlenesses of humanity, and made to feel the puerility of the petty objects which set men's interests at variance, contrasted with the nobler pleasures which all might share.[22]

The experience of nature has such power because it presents us with the feeling of nature as a kingdom independent of us. In order to account for this independence, Mill reaches back to the teleological vocabulary. As he writes: "Solitude, in the sense of being often alone, is essential to any depth of meditation or of character; and solitude in the presence of natural beauty and grandeur, is the cradle of thoughts and aspirations which are not only good for the individual, but which society could ill do without. Nor is there much satisfaction in contemplating the world with nothing left to the spontaneous activity of nature."[23] Here we can appreciate once again how Mill is not so much concerned with the elimination of the teleological framework as such, but rather with testing its role in relation to the primary moral work. He identifies such a role in the region of experience in which beauty puts us in touch with the sentiment of independence of organisms and natural environments. This particular experience has the capacity to bring us back in touch with the overall fabric of the universe that nourishes our imagination and diverts us from the selfishness and pettiness of our interests. The area occupied by teleology in the traditional framework is revisited by Mill—and not debunked as in the skeptical Enlightenment model—, and eventually refitted in the novel modern framework as a key component of the education and transformation of one's self.[24]

5.4 Experimenting with individuality

With Mill, a society that treasures freedom and subjectivity is one that works to create the best conditions possible for engaging in the struggle for individuality. As he writes:

> where, not the person's own character, but the traditions or customs of other people are the rule of conduct, there is wanting one of the principal ingredients of human happiness, and quite the chief ingredient of individual and social progress.[25]

The beliefs and conducts chosen in the shadow of liberal warranties, which do not actively involve the self, tend to extinguish and distort themselves. The situation Mill deprecates in his society is precisely one in which

> even in what people do for pleasure, conformity is the first thing thought of; they like in crowds; they exercise choice only among things commonly done: peculiarity of taste, eccentricity of conduct, are shunned equally with crimes: until by dint of not following their own nature, they have no nature to follow: their human capacities

> are withered and starved: they become incapable of any strong wishes or native pleasures, and are generally without either opinions or feelings of home growth, or properly their own.[26]

We can thus integrate the circle of opponents of freedom. Its opponents are the ones I have listed in this book: the traditional picture and those conceptions that restrict human potentialities to the scientific-technical dimension. There is, however, yet one more opponent, which insinuates itself into the very texture of freedom and which consists in the transformation of ways of living designed to encourage opportunities for freedom into ways of confining individual life in conceptions and conducts that are merely passively absorbed. We can appreciate this new enemy of freedom if we consider the latter from the point of view of the relationship the self is able to establish with itself, with its beliefs, pleasures, and conducts—a relationship that can either make subjectivity bloom or produce subjection, as both Mill and Foucault showed us. If we picture freedom and subjectivity as the effects of the primary moral work with which we give form to ourselves, we may acknowledge that they are not secured once for all and that their unexpected enemy lies in our condescendingly putting something aside as a safe conquest, even if it was achieved in terms of freedom and individual interests. I have begun the book with this theme, asking myself why we should rethink the achievements of modern democratic societies on the themes of human life. We now know that no achievement can simply be taken for granted ever, as something secured once for all.

Let me mention a few examples. Think of the experiments in the sexual revolution at the beginning of last century that have faded, not only because of the Nazi or communist oppression—or even as a result of milder democratic shifts, as in the conservative change of direction in the United States—but, closer to us, by having transformed what was novel and experimental into something merely conventional, chosen in conformity with the majority. Think of feminism, of the discovery of the fresh and novel voice of women heard for the first time—with Marguerite Duras: after centuries of oppression, "the woman is now young, fresh"[27]—and of the difficulties of keeping such a voice alive and new. As the Italian feminist theorist Carla Lonzi wrote: "women's difference consists in millenniums of absence from history. Let us make the best of difference: once the admission of the woman is achieved, who can tell how many millenniums would it take to shake off this new yoke?"[28] But think also of the apparently conservative position held by Mary Warnock, when she writes that the acquisitions in terms of reproductive freedom may lead to the loss of "the old sense of astonishment and gratitude that came from the birth of a child".[29] A statement which could also be read as the cry for the loss of the sort of joy at what belongs to us as something intimate and deep, which should not be taken for granted and which should strike people in ever new and unexpected ways. In a similar way, the danger, voiced by some, that euthanasia would become a hasty practice covering up the shortcomings of society[30] might also be read as the fear that we might lose the sense in which we are confronting here a personal and profound choice, drawing on our entire existence—as shown in notable movies such as *The Barbarian Invasions* by George-Henri Denys Arcand (2003) and *The Sea Inside* by Alejandro Amenábar (2004).

In conclusion, Mill helps us to draw a complex and fertile picture. We have the direct opponents of freedom—the traditional conceptions and those granting exclusive privilege to science and technology—and then there is the need to secure forms of life that engage our person and relations in their entirety. If we consider this latter problem for freedom, along with the former two, we can then realize how all that takes place center stage is always on the verge of fading and losing its association with existence in its entirety. We are thus in the vital need of areas where we can experiment with life in ever new ways, with marginal areas, peripheral zones far from the center, even when the center is represented by the fundamental values of personal freedom and the promotion of the general interest. If the forms that have secured freedom are always on the verge of turning into cages for freedom itself, forms which put at the center opinions, choices, sentiments, pleasures, and conducts that merely await to be absorbed rather than won over every time, we are then in need of finding ever new conditions through which to engage in the perpetual struggle of the margin with the center, the struggle for individuality.

Notes

1 Michel Foucault, *Security, Territory, Population*, op. cit., p. 231, notes how "Western man is individualized through the pastorate insofar as the pastorate leads him to his salvation that fixes his identity for eternity, subjects him to a network of unconditional obedience."

2 Søren Kierkegaard, *Fear and Trembling*, London: Penguin Classics, 1985. On the other hand, Kierkegaard also writes that morality would not be abolished but only revisited through the notion of paradox: *ibid.*, p. 89.

3 Michel Foucault, *Security, Territory, Population*, op. cit.

4 G.E.M. Anscombe, "You Can Have Sex Without Children. Christianity and the New Offer," in *Ethics, Religion and Politics*, op. cit., pp. 82–96.

5 John McDowell, "Eudaimonism and Realism in Aristotle's Ethics," in *The Engaged Intellect*, op. cit., pp. 29–30.
6 For a treatment of sexuality along these lines, see Richard Posner, *Sex and Reason*, Cambridge (MA): Harvard University Press, 1992.
7 The reference is once again to Foucault's work. For the concept of psychoanalytic normality, see *Abnormal*, op. cit.; for the concept of normality tied to the social sciences, see *The Birth of the Biopolitics*, op. cit. On the example of sexuality, see David M. Halperin, *What Do Gay Men Want? An Essay on Sex, Risk, and Subjectivity*, Ann Arbor: The University of Michigan Press, 2007.
8 Michel Foucault, "The Ethics of the Concern for the Self as a Practice of Freedom," in *The Essential Works of Michel Foucault 1954–1984*, op. cit., pp. 283–284.
9 Michel Foucault, *The Birth of the Biopolitics*, op. cit., lecture of 4 April 1979; see also the two alternatives to sovereign power—the revolutionary and Rousseauian one and that of British philosophical radicalism.
10 For an interpretation, see Piergiorgio Donatelli, *Introduzione a John Stuart Mill*, op. cit. On Cavell on Mill, see Stanley Cavell, *Cities of Words. Pedagogical Letters on a Register of the Moral Life*, Cambridge (MA): Harvard University Press, 2004, pp. 82–101.
11 John Stuart Mill, *A System of Logic Ratiocinative and Inductive*, in *Collected Works of John Stuart Mill*, Vol. VIII, ed. by J.M. Robson, Toronto: University of Toronto Press, 1974, p. 952.
12 John Stuart Mill, *On Liberty*, op. cit., Chapter 1.
13 *Ibid.*, p. 224: "It is proper to state that I forego any advantage which could be derived to my argument from the idea of abstract right, as a thing independent of utility. I regard utility as the ultimate appeal on all ethical questions: but it must be utility in the largest sense, grounded on the permanent interests of man as a progressive being."
14 John Stuart Mill, *Autobiography*, in *Collected Works of John Stuart Mill*, Vol. I: *Autobiography and Literary Essays*, ed. by J.M. Robson, Toronto: University of Toronto Press, 1981, p. 146.
15 For the role of the Roman Church in the Middle Ages, see John Stuart Mill, "Michelet's History of France" (1844), in *Essays on French History and Historians*, op. cit., p. 247. On the role of the Reformation, see *On Liberty*, op. cit., Chapter 2; on the revision of the role of religion, see "The Utility of Religion," in *Collected Works of John Stuart Mill*, Vol. X: *Essays on Ethics, Religion and Society*, op. cit.
16 J.S. Mill, *On Liberty*, op. cit., p. 242.
17 *Ibid.*, p. 255.
18 John Stuart Mill, "Theism," in *Collected Works of John Stuart Mill*, Vol. 10: *Essays on Ethics, Religion and Society*, op. cit.
19 John Stuart Mill, "Inaugural Address to the University of St. Andrews," in *Collected Works of John Stuart Mill*, Vol. XXI: *Essays on Equality, Law, and Education*, op. cit.
20 John Stuart Mill, *On Liberty*, op. cit., pp. 301–302.
21 John Stuart Mill, "Nature," in *Collected Works of John Stuart Mill*, Vol. X: *Essays on Ethics, Religion and Society*, op. cit.
22 John Stuart Mill, "Inaugural Address to the University of St. Andrews," op. cit., p. 255.

23 John Stuart Mill, *Principles of Political Economy, with Chapters on Socialism*, ed. by Jonathan Riley, Oxford: Oxford University Press, 2008, p. 129.
24 On this theme, see Piergiorgio Donatelli, "The Environment and the Background of Human Life. Nature, Facts and Values," in *Facts and Values. The Ethics and Metaphysics of Normativity*, ed. by G. Marchetti and S. Marchetti, New York: Routledge, 2017, pp. 246–263.
25 John Stuart Mill, *On Liberty*, op. cit., p. 261.
26 *Ibid.*, p. 265.
27 Marguerite Duras, *La vie matérielle*, Paris: POL, 1987.
28 Carla Lonzi, *Sputiamo su Hegel e altri scritti* (1974), Milano: et al./edizioni, 2010, p. 15.
29 Mary Warnock, *Making Babies: Is There a Right to Have Children?*, Oxford: Oxford University Press, 2002, p. 113.
30 See the views held by Sissela Bok, in G. Dworkin, R.G. Frey and S. Bok, *Euthanasia and Physician–Assisted Suicide*, Cambridge: Cambridge University Press, 1998.

Chapter 6

Sexuality, reproduction, death

6.1 What makes us human?

I have spoken of sexuality, reproduction, and death as crucial places for verifying the character of human life from the vantage point of view of freedom: they are places where we can assess whether human life is experienced as freedom or rather as conforming to something that comes from without. Now, one might ask, why these areas in the first place? In order to answer this question, we should go back once more to the traditional conception as expressed along the three canonical axes we examined. In the traditional picture, these are the constitutive areas of human nature. We are human beings because we are born, die, and have sex in determinate ways. For example, being born from the body of a woman, as part of a process in which a design is revealed that is honored by the woman through her respect and reverence, which is part of her duties to the conjugal relation within the institution of marriage, is one of the constitutive features of our humanity.

The moral considerations regarding these ways of life thus have the aspect of absolute prohibitions: that is, they prohibit actions that if performed would reveal the lack of acknowledgment of one's humanity (Chapter 2, §2.5.3). Absolute prohibitions are what characterize the proper form in which the divine law is expressed but are at the same time the ways to signal those features of human life without which the entire framework would fall apart. Furthermore, absolute prohibitions charge the body with meanings; they are the expression of the kind of constraint generated by our very perception of the human body. Therefore, in the traditional picture, the three axes contribute to making the various features of human life the constitutive areas of our humanity. The traditional picture and the conservative stances furthering it nowadays present the three areas precisely in these terms: in their perspective, these are not simply some of the areas to which virtues apply but are the defining areas of our very humanity. In this sense, Aquinas speaks of the transgressions of certain duties in sexual matters as sins against nature and grants them the power to dispel the entire divine order of nature.[1] In the elaboration of perfect duties toward one's bodily nature—from which the prohibition of suicide, bodily maiming, and bestiality is derived—Kant gives voice to this very same tradition of natural law, which surfaces in certain moments of his thought that elude the overall layout of his conception, which is committed to the criticism of metaphysics even in this particular variety. His language is in fact that of the horror felt when facing the transgression of absolute duties, a horror generated by the perception of the subversion of the natural order—that is, of the way in which the natural order is the expression of the intrinsic moral order. He writes: "the most serious violations of the duties to oneself produce either revulsion with horror, and such is suicide, or revulsion with disgust, and such are the *crimina carnis*."[2]

The idea that there are areas of human life constitutive of our humanity is then part and parcel of the traditional picture. In such a picture, the prospect of choice at the outset of life, the separation between sexuality and reproduction, the overcoming of the male/female dichotomy, or dying as a process fraught with choice are all possibilities deemed as against nature, that is, possibilities whose realization would jeopardize the entire human framework at once. As we saw, Anscombe speaks in these terms, pulling all these new forms of freedom in these areas of life together and equating them to a situation in which what took place was in effect an attempt to subvert the most basic human framework: namely, Nazism.

The fall of the traditional picture, with the establishment of the central lines of modern moral culture, made it harder and harder to advance this kind of arguments, and this partially explains the somewhat artificial ring they have nowadays. How can we in fact sensibly claim that the new techniques of medically assisted reproduction, sexual freedom, or the new forms of choice at the end of life make the societies that have welcomed them akin to the Nazi one? It is no surprise, then, that in recent years the conservative positions have been reframed and, for example, at the beginning of life they defend the list of their prohibitions by referring to the rights of the embryo considered as a person. The language of rights is part of current living culture, it is the result of the moral culture of the Enlightenment, even if the use made of it by the conservatives betrays the spirit of the original enterprise: it is in fact a completely instrumental use since the very notion of rights makes sense if applied to individuals who clearly are persons. And yet it is a parasitic use of a language which is alive, whereas the language of the subversion of the natural order represents a fairly coherent use of a framework that has disappeared.

Therefore, in the framework of modern moral culture, reflection on what makes these areas of human life crucial and salient in the first place has gradually abandoned the language of constitutive features. The contrast between the traditional and the modern picture, therefore, has also the following distinctive characteristic: namely, it is not only a matter of having brought these areas into the human scene of freedom and subjectivity. The consequence was that the possibility to think of them as constitutive was lost and with it to think of them in terms of sins against nature, of the subversion of the moral order, of what is monstrous, and of absolute prohibitions. In the traditional understanding, being human meant considering sexuality, reproduction, and death as areas governed by absolute duties and prohibitions. These duties and prohibitions indicate the conducts in which the essential features of the human form of life are articulated. We are humans because sexuality, reproduction, and dying describe us in our essential characteristics, and do so in determinate ways. Absolute duties and prohibitions mark such determinate ways. It is thus clear that the disappearance of the background that allowed to weave together a certain area of life around specific modalities—e.g., we are human beings because we are born, and birth is the result of the process of reproduction; there are determinate ways in which one reproduces, involving those sexual capacities and appetites revealing our humanity, and which are also the objects of the conjugal duties—also means transforming that area of life, not only eroding the duties and prohibitions featuring it. It is the entire area of life that changes. In Foucault's language, it is not only the code that changes but also how we problematize a certain area of life in the first place.[3]

As I have been claiming, influential defenders of Enlightenment and of liberal modernity are ill-suited to acknowledging this point as they picture their victories only in terms of the dissolution of the traditional framework, on the one hand, and of the affirmation of the concepts of freedom and interests, on the other, conceived of as operating on separate planes. In this way, they do not see that the areas of human life that go beyond the traditional picture have been reshaped according to different frameworks, different ways of living, which make the exercise of freedom more or less hospitable and congenial. In this way, as I have argued, they are equally blind to new rivals, including the new ways in which specialized medical and technological dispositives take over these areas of life to fulfill their interests, which are only a partial set of our interests.

From the point of view of the liberal conceptions working on universal principles and leaving to science and technology with the task of giving an account of the world on which moral considerations operate, one might have the impression that the defeat of the traditional picture was followed by the crumbling of the resources that made sexuality, reproduction, and dying constitutive areas shaped by absolute duties and prohibitions—among which are the prohibitions on abortion, suicide, and sexual conducts other than those that have in view procreation within the traditional understanding of marriage. In this perspective, it seems that this defeat would hand these areas of life over to liberties and interests, that is to say, over to the operation of the liberal principles. However, this view is simply blind to the fact that having removed the traditional picture does not impede other frameworks from taking over these areas (partially at least) and making their influence felt by shaping the moral possibilities of thought, experience, and action. Foucault's analysis of the crucial scene of psychiatry and more generally of the social sciences of the eighteenth-century has shown how the impression that the eclipse of the Christian framework would hand the scene over to the neutral framework of science—which allowed the free expression of individual choices—proved to be misguided. In his account, in fact, what psychiatry and the social sciences present us with as sexuality, for example, is a field fraught with meanings, interests, techniques, and relations which shape pretty much exhaustively what we can do, and it does this by imposing new conformities and new forms of oppression. Furthermore, he claims that this field is equally the result of the confluence of previous conceptualizations, as I have mentioned above. Therefore, it is naïve to think that a framework such as the Christian or "pastoral" one, which has deeply affected sexuality and human life generally, could leave the space it occupied for many centuries empty, as a frictionless surface for the modern moral principles to operate. The point is a general one, as we saw: we should not hide from view the ways in which facts, perceptions, relations, and techniques generate an area of life in which we do things with knowledge, action and experience. The traditional picture was one of these ways: complex, articulated, and long-lasting. Its gradual demise leaves the space for other ways, other frameworks.

I would now like to briefly suggest how to rethink the three areas of life in this perspective, that is, as modes of experience that have undergone transformation, emancipating us from the traditional picture and now inhabiting the modern world at the crossroads of these diverse interests, of the new resistances of the conservatives, of the new forms of normalization, and as an expression of a liberal and democratic life that is often unequipped to understand itself.

6.2 Sexuality

In the area of sexuality, it is possible to fully assess the ruinous fall of the traditional framework. Over the centuries, this framework was able to assemble together—along the three axes we have considered—sexual experience, the role of male and female genders, their stabilization in the family setting, and reproduction. It produced the conditions for taking this experience as natural, as what escapes the mutability of customs and human history. An area such as sexuality, of which in the variety of their historical situations human beings have done largely different things, was shaped and presented as one in which it seemed that our nature spoke in its deepest and universal voice, a voice that could express the unbreakable foundation of humanity: in this way, sexuality became a crucial moment of Christian anthropology. The soldering of the three aspects referred to—sexual experience, the dichotomy of male and female, and reproduction—was obtained in this way, and we find it once again in contemporary conservative advocates such as Anscombe. Humanity is thought of in dichotomic terms as masculine or feminine. In turn, this dichotomy gets its meaning from the fulfillment of the reproductive dimension, which finds its appropriate context in marriage. In this light, sexuality is seen exclusively in reproductive terms: it regards the reproductive union of a male with a female in the properly human context of marriage.

The centuries-long history of the truly extraordinary successful attempt to cage the human variety belonging to each of the three aspects within a unitary picture is genuinely fascinating: how it was possible to curb the variety of ways in which we are sexual beings and the variety of things we do with sex, apart from engaging in reproduction. It is a history in which, as we have seen, all the elements capable of generating a framework are recruited. In Foucault's perspective, the connection between sexuality and reproduction is not sufficient to account for the process that gradually made sexuality something personal and intimate, and, at the end of the road, a hardly avoidable feature of our identity as it is nowadays: a truly unthinkable outcome for the Greeks. This took place thanks to the narrower and narrower controls which Christianity implemented on conducts first, and then on thoughts and the most intimate aspects of imagination.[4] It is not my intention to sum up this history, but I would like to evoke it with a line—which we can gather, once again, from Foucault. At the moment when the struggles to confine human beings within marriage and family began to bear their fruits, when the nineteenth-century bourgeoisie had some widespread affluence and a capillary structure of social powers involved a significant number of people, in such apical moment of social pressure around the family unit, the latter exploded and we needed psychiatry and, in particular, the new psychoanalysis to take care of these individuals that the new claustrophobic dimension of marriage and family made so unstable and fragile!

What I would like to comment on is, rather, the subsequent history, that which has seen the much-aspired-to unity of the three aspects of the traditional picture crumble as a result of the central lines of modern moral culture, which, with the crumbling of teleology, the divine law, and the widespread social conceptions about roles and activities tied to sexuality, has eroded the ground on which the astounding construction of the family was erected. This was a rather discontinuous history. In effect, sexual experience seems to be particularly open to permanent changes and rearrangements. We could think of the sexual experimentations in Berlin between the two wars, in Russia before the revolution, later on in Cuba, or in New York early in the past century, already reaching a maturity of contents which were wiped out by dictatorships or by the softer counterforces in democracy. Instead, these contents reached stability in the sexual revolution that took place within a decade in Sweden across the fifties and sixties, and which gradually grew subsequently in democratic countries.

With the fading of the traditional picture, the unity of these aspects has been broken by the important progress achieved within the discontinuous history of the twentieth century, and these aspects have been transformed following their separation. The gender dichotomy has fallen apart, and the equation of sexuality with reproduction equally. This has deeply affected the concepts of gender, sexuality and reproduction. What it means to be a woman in the first place has changed, and this change has introduced the concepts of sexual identity and orientation: it introduced sexuality as a personal experience tied to subjectivity; it introduced reproduction as a woman's choice and hence returned it to the whole of humanity in such a form.

I would now like to draw some considerations on the possibilities opened by the new framework in which sexual experience now lives. Then, in the spirit of this book, I shall gesture at what is disclosed for us in light of the liberal and democratic acquisitions in this area, which includes not only the freedom to have sex between consenting adults in whatever way one sees fit but also the introduction of new juridical institutions, such as the extension of marriage to same-sex couples and the institution of diverse types of civil unions. As I have underlined a number of times, the question of the construction of one's subjectivity in the various areas of life, that is, the issue of the sedimentation of a hospitable soil for the creative exercise of the self, presupposes that the struggle for the liberation from oppression characteristic of the traditional picture has been achieved already. Once secured, a number of possibilities are disclosed. These are the possibilities we face in the many democratic societies that have secured these acquisitions.

It seems to me that the chance to transform sexuality into a field in which to experiment with one's subjectivity is still largely unexplored. The moment we pulled sexuality out of the traditional picture and emancipated it both from a binary conception of humanity (in terms of males and females) and reproduction, it started looking like an original field of experience, a field that requires a new understanding. What becomes possibile now is the chance to consolidate a scene in which sexuality is a way to create relationships, pleasures, and experiences in the light of freedom. All this depends on effective experimentation, on having groups that experiment with and consolidate experience in modalities that are inclusive of people, and societies wise enough to let these experimentations circulate and provide instruction. In this sense, the two movements, groups, and key sites for reflection on the sexual liberation, those represented by feminism and LGBT communities, prove to be pivotal.

Breaking free of the traditional picture has transformed the dichotomy of genders into a pluralism of genders and sexual orientations. The struggles for liberation, feminist and LGBT alike, re-employed the invention of psychiatric and psychological identity in order to overturn it and claim spaces of life and freedom. But now the issue we face, which is the issue Foucault also faced, is if to keep thinking of sexuality as an identity, as a form of human life in which to identify ourselves, is indeed congenial to the formation of ways of living in which to freely cultivate ourselves.[5] On the one hand, there certainly are sexual identities, and I have stressed the importance of being able to claim these *realities* so as to be able to affirm oneself and one's subjectivity (Chapter 4, §4.4). On the other hand, the notion of identity might prove to be a way of actually exhausting the potentialities of the sexual sphere. This can be appreciated if we consider two aspects: namely, relations and pleasures.

On certain occasions, at moments in which we treasure this kind of experience, sexual relationships allow for an intimate connection with strangers while remaining also strangers to ourselves.[6] Sexual relationships have the power—which other forms of relationships lack, at least to the same degree—to put us in a position to experiment with relationships in which our identity and the identity of our partners are left in the shadow or at any rate do not play a central role and do not determine the form of the relation itself. Rich and intimate sexual encounters with strangers are a clear case of such experimentation, but we could think that this potential belongs to sexuality as such, even in the encounter with one's partner: a kind of encounter in which the relationship betrays aspects of the other and oneself that are not determined by one's identity, which, on the other hand, pervades all the other aspects of our life and contributes to the definition of one's character—hence, representing the bases of the exercise of one's faculties in free and creative ways. In the cases at hand, by contrast, a different kind of creativity might be in place. A comparison might be drawn with what Kant writes about the judgment of taste: in the experience of taste, we are as it were more free, more creative, than in the sphere of morals, which, however, he defines as the sphere of freedom. There is a freedom that invents its rules after applying them, a freedom in which what we experience is the opportunity to establish rules that could not have been anticipated.[7]

The notion of sexual identity—which represents the current stage of the criticism advanced both to the traditional picture and to the psychiatrization and psychologization of sexuality—allowed for, and is itself the expression of, ways of life that produced freedom in the first place: but we can now start to notice the limits which these modalities place upon this area of our existence. It was and it still is all-important that people discovered and experienced themselves as, say, a woman in the sense in which this existential condition envisages spaces of movement that we thought precluded and that reveal themselves once the old framework has changed dramatically; the same goes with discovering oneself and experiencing oneself as gay or lesbian, say, or rather experiencing and discovering a tension with one's body that turns out to be the discovery of the need for a transition, which is itself open to a rich variety of identities and perceptions of the self. These kinds of discoveries are part of processes of strengthening of the self which are crucial on the path to becoming subjects. The possibility of becoming subjects requires stable forms of identification with ourselves, which, in turn, consolidate in one's character. But we also know, from Mill, that what we have so acquired and that we are willing to take for granted has the inner tendency to die out. This holds for all the spheres of our interests. Yet there are potentialities that belong to sexuality especially, that live exclusively in the space created by the oblivion of our identity, and which, as such, travel at a significant distance from other forms of subjective interests and preferences.

The possibility of experimenting with this form of experience of the self and others depends on an entire world of relations, perceptions, attitudes, and spaces of social life. This world has been secured, but its fiber is indeed fragile. The sphere of sexual relationships undergoes a number of considerable pressures, which I have indicated and to which we can add a specific social pressure: the interest in stable forms of life, in the family particularly, as a nucleus of relations constituting the intersection of crucial economic and social interests such as wealth, well-being, and political stability. I have argued how scientific and technological interests prove to be of great value for us, but we could well criticize the perspective that treats them as the only interests pertaining to a certain area of human life. Analogously, we can criticize the idea that social and economic interests—having to do, for example, with the family—exhaust the meaning of intimate relationships.

The very idea of sexuality—now understood as the field of experimentation of that particular kind of subjectivity that admits goods which would be lost without creating the specific conditions in which such subjectivity could be expressed—can be further articulated with the introduction of the theme of pleasures. What are sexual pleasures? What does it mean to bring the concept of pleasure outside of the traditional picture, and also of the psychological perspective, and lead it to a dimension in which what is at stake is not our identity and in which, precisely because of that, we richly and fully exercise our subjectivity? The question, which regards the specific ways of life with which we are able to experiment and that we may eventually weave together, is, then, the following: what is left once sexual pleasure is disconnected from the traditional picture, where it had a role tied to the generative relationship between the sexes, and from the psychological picture, in which it is related to psychical dynamics to be discovered and studied in the light of a notion of normality, of taxonomical and practical interests? In Mill's and Foucault's perspective, pleasures are what we experiment with from within forms of experience we have educated and to which we have dedicated our attention. If these forms of experience and relationship are thought of as the kind of intimate contact through which we get in touch with the sides of ourselves and others that are left in the shade, pleasure becomes the spark kindled by the very experimentation with these sides left in the shade. Pleasure no longer belongs anymore to the reproductive relationship, as happened in the traditional picture, nor to the new scene of normality represented in psychological terms, but is rather the form in which we experiment with the encounter with the unknown side of ourselves and others or, as we could say, with the encounter with ourselves and others in the form of an intimate encounter between strangers.

In this perspective, sexual pleasures belong to a modality of the constitution of the self as subject; they are considered in the light of these goals rather than those of medicine, psychology, or of economic and social interests. On the other hand, the basis by which we distinguish them from other pleasures shifts. Once detached from both reproduction and psychologization, disjointed from the framework of the family and from economic taxonomies of conducts, pleasures start looking like those that Mill called aesthetic pleasures, thanks to which we transform the texture of our being and work on the imagination. These specific aesthetic pleasures, though, are blessed with the feature I have pointed out: namely, they generate an intimacy that presents others and ourselves in ever new and unknown forms, having the power to radically interrogate the acquired sense of the self.

6.3 Reproduction

Considered from the contemporary scene—where the traditional picture has fallen apart and liberties and rights have been secured—as with sexuality, the issue of reproduction looks like a totally unprecedented area of experimentation of subjectivity. With the fading of the traditional picture and with reproduction handed to women and their choices, the road ahead consists in the articulation of the space of women's subjectivity. This will in turn transform the fact and meaning of reproduction for us all. This task, which consists of recruiting enough resources to secure a framework in which reproduction appears as the exercise of the subjectivity of women, has notable opponents in medical and social interests toward reproduction. The space of subjectivity now seems restricted to choosing whether to reproduce or not, which extends to the choice of whether to interrupt pregnancy, leaving the entire reproductive path in the hands of medical and social interests that take it over and rule it from their perspective. From the point of view of medical technology, of social medicine, and what gets represented through medical examinations, screenings, and the results of the analyses of risky conducts, this entire scene of descriptions, interests, and attitudes tends to deposit a conception of reproduction that excludes the possibility, for women, of taking it over as an aspect of their lives in which to freely experiment with themselves.

Those liberal views disinterested in the wider frameworks in which it makes sense to freely choose and live do not see the problem at all; actually, they might turn out to be unwitting allies of these forms of dispossession of women's freedom. In the liberal picture, reproduction is considered from the point of view of the choice and the responsibility of women and of the people involved in view of the consequences of these choices. But if we narrow down the scope of choice to the yes or no to pregnancy and to the ways in which this decision can take shape, and at the same time we leave medicine and the social interests to health to take over the reproductive process, the defense of the liberal framework might bring with it the exclusion of reproduction as an appropriate locus for the expression of freedom. What is happening is that the defense of women's freedom without contents, without anthropological bases, matched with the transformation of reproduction into a place of medical and technological intervention in the light of health and social interests,[8] is depositing enough resources to successfully invite us to think of the pregnant body as a fetal container. In a context in which pregnancy is increasingly seen as a process in which technology has the lion's share, it tends to be seen in the shadow of the concept of ectogenesis. It is as if we considered women's pregnancy as more and more a biological variety of the artificial womb, and pregnant women as biological instances of the ectogenetic model of pregnancy. A woman's body is now part of a complex web of medical and pharmacological interventions, pervaded by diagnostic techniques, which increasingly makes it easy to think of it as a biological instrument.

I have offered a rather extreme depiction of the current state of affairs in order to highlight a fundamental conceptual contrast. The fall of the traditional picture and the defense of freedom without anthropological bases leave reproduction as a terrain which is up for grabs and claimed by all sorts of interests—for example, and most notably, interests for the well-being of the unborn, which we subscribe only to realize how the moment such interests exhaust the perception of pregnancy, they become ways of cementing a scene in which once again women's freedom is cancelled.

The diagnosis I have offered might help to understand the complex situation where the defense of women stands now, even for feminist thinkers. The criticism of the transformation of a woman's body into a biological-technological device might throw a favorable light on the traditional picture, which represented pregnancy as a process to honor, fostering in this way a convergence with the conservative arguments denouncing the medical technologies at the beginning of life as a way of turning reproduction into a mechanical process. And yet we know that the traditional picture defends a background that has no room for women's freedom. That picture and present-day conservative stances might seem appealing only if we are blind to a further road that escapes the alternative between the traditional view which sees ends and intangible processes to honor and the background partially deposited by current liberal and technological societies that exhaustively medicalize pregnancy. The further road is that of making the entire process of pregnancy a matter of freedom or, vice-versa, to think of freedom as what might be exercised from the point of view of the first-person experience of women experiencing pregnancy.

At the same time, we also know that, facing the fall of the traditional picture, present-day conservatives take an alternative path, which is that of defending traditional prohibitions via the language of modernity, and in particular of rights. They do not speak the language of a teleology to honor, in which the divine design and its law are revealed, as this is shown in the perception of the woman's body as an object of chastity and reverence: they speak the rather different language and arguments of rights. The traditional range of prohibitions and the battle against reproductive freedom are defended as ways of protecting the rights of the embryo-person, which covers its path from conception to birth within the body-container of the woman. These conservatives may thus find an ally in the technological liberal society. From their point of view, with the impossibility of appealing to the virtue of chastity, to the prohibition on transgressing the intrinsic moral order to which we are liable when intervening on pregnancy, it is to their advantage that modern society transforms pregnancy into the place of the formation of the fetus, which we can monitor through diagnostic instruments and check on the progress in the context of a completely medicalized notion and practice of pregnancy which takes for granted that women entrust their bodies to medical structures. As a matter of fact, the present-day context might appear a very convenient one for these new conservatives, as it presents them with a congenial terrain from which to launch a defense of the rights of the embryo and to distort—as is to be expected from those conservatives employing the liberal language only opportunistically—individual and social responsibility toward the unborn as ways of debunking the space of freedom for women.

For these reasons, I believe that the space of women's subjectivity in reproduction is largely new. The possibility of establishing a framework in which reproduction is a territory entirely annexed to women's subjectivity represents an important change for everybody. We thus need to start thinking of reproduction as something that a portion of humanity autonomously decides to pursue: women nowadays, but we may already think of gestation carried through by transgender men, and largely unexplored possibilities come into view—possibilities in the near future that will open up to the chances of freedom and happiness and to the risks now only involving women. The idea of reproductive freedom freed of both the traditional conception of teleological ends and the modern medical one discloses a radical sense of subjectivity. Pregnancy becomes, in effect, a vast and indefinite series of choices: the choices that constitute the texture of the lives of pregnant women. If we free reproduction of the sense of necessity which it has already escaped—the one pertaining to the metaphysics of generative teleology—and free it of the new sense of medical necessity and return it to the freedom of women's choices, a scenario opens up in which we can rethink a number of issues in ever more fruitful ways.

Reproduction, understood as this kind of sphere of life, makes giving birth to babies a matter of free choice based on the elaboration of subjectivities and hence on the creativity of the subjects involved. They are not choices where the goal is that of conforming to the necessities of life and society, choices in which the individual only gets to express herself in her contribution to processes that do not belong to her personally. Here we—women in the first place and hence all of us—have instead the chance to appropriate pregnancy as something in which the entire texture of subjectivity is involved. In this way, we can free the activity of making and raising babies from necessity—in its various forms: metaphysical, medical, social—and hand these activities back to subjectivity. As Carla Lonzi writes, "should they not see us as the continuers of the species. We give children to no one, neither to men nor to the state. We give them to themselves and return ourselves to ourselves."[9] In this way, by intensifying subjectivity, we radicalize the degree of moral investment as well: what we do here comes from us and hence it involves the self radically. This in effect is the scenario that is made possibile in those still new situations in which reproduction is tied to choice. Gay and lesbian couples with children live in situations in which reproduction appears as something extraordinary, affecting them in radical ways. They are finding out as it were for the first time the gigantic meaning, the beauty, and the tremendous responsibility of bringing babies into the world and raising them. This is the kind of moral radicalization that might well follow from bringing reproduction within the scope of women's subjectivity, removing it from the sense of necessity, and returning it in this manner to all of us. The chance is that of being able to transform these areas of life into fresh and novel conducts, sentiments, choices, activities, and situations driven by the sense of a living possibility.

A whole range of issues can be reshaped by this radical sense of open possibility and moral involvement. One of these is the choice of whether to accept a pregnancy and the multiple choices women take afterward, among which is that of what to do once the baby is born: whether to keep her or rather give her up for adoption—a choice taken before conception, during pregnancy, but also at birth. Among these, within the context of the radicalization of freedom and of moral responsibility I am hinting at, surrogacy appears potentially as a meaningful and rich choice: having an experience of maternity, of giving one's newborn baby, and establishing relationships with those that embrace her as their own child. A scenario already legally at home in some countries, though I would like here to point out, in the Millian spirit of this book, its underlying framework: that is, what these laws and regulations make possible in terms of personal and relational experiences, and of the form that a society welcoming such practices would take. It is surely inadequate to picture surrogacy as such as a form of exploitation of women, even if this is precisely the situation with many women involved in this practice. As we know, the contrast between pregnancy as a locus of thick meanings to honor and pregnancy as a mere instrument is the result of the opposition that I have been criticizing throughout the book and which neglects an alternative perspective: that is, that of abandoning the traditional picture and building up different meanings, perceptions, and concerns which pave the way for previously unthinkable choices. In the traditional picture, respect was paid to women as they engaged in an activity to which they did not contribute with their subjectivities; while respect is now paid (and similar moral sentiments) to the subjective dedication of women toward an activity which is still fraught with meaning: that is, the coming into the world of new human beings. In this light, considering surrogacy as a rich and conscientious moral choice signals the emergence of a new moral scene, which has radicalized the subjective character of reproduction and has at the same time revised and intensified the gratitude and responsibility we owe to those taking up the burden of reproduction, precisely because these choices are no longer seen as necessary (that is, as what is part of women's duties). It is only insofar as we have radicalized women's freedom and the responsibility for an action that is in no way due that we are able to see surrogacy as a good choice.

A rather different question is that of raising children and parenthood. These practices are highly influenced by how we think of the family and hence the role of the genders in it but it is equally influenced by the transformation of the scene of reproduction. To radicalize the subjectivity of reproduction also affects the education of children as an issue that opens up the subjectivity of the people involved. We have secured a number of achievements—employing the "we" on the assumption of the wider perspective of imagination defended in this book—such as adoption by couples and singles, and surrogacy, the equality of the partners, the rights of children, and so on. But, to be sure, the chance of divorcing the being and acting as parents from the traditional picture and at the same time from the new scenes of normalization, and, instead, connecting them to the exercise of subjectivity, seems completely new to me. As I have already observed, family roles are those most easily characterized by conceptions that are not felt in need of being critically scrutinized, in which we prove to be most indulgent and passive. By sharing and expanding our experiences, we now have the resources for wide-ranging experimentation with what it means to educate ourselves and others into becoming subjects: that is, people who fully exercise their freedom, thus rethinking in this new scenario the distinctive and constitutive asymmetries of age, maturity, authority, responsibility, and so on that are involved in the activity of being mothers and fathers.

6.4 Death

The possibility of securing personal and creative ways of life with regard to our own death seems to occupy the very same kind of uncertain space that is also characteristic of reproduction. A few observations are in order. In this field too we can reflect on the situation that is disclosed once freedom and rights have been secured, and hence the possibility of expressing one's refusal of medical treatments as well as the possibility of being helped to die in determinate conditions once we request so with the active intervention of medical personnel. Once these liberties and rights have been secured and guaranteed, we may envisage a complicated and rich space of opportunities made possible and yet also difficult by the medicalization of the dying process. The new ways of dying pervade the final part of life with technology and in particular with life-support machines that allow the process to continue indefinitely. Medicalized death is one of the crucial facts that has contributed to the crumbling of the traditional framework, in which the attitudes of respect and reverence for the solemnity of death, where one could envisage a design and a teleology higher than individual wishes and interests, were anchored to the fact that death was out of our control—with perhaps the only specific exception of anticipating it with the choice of suicide. The medicalization of dying shattered this background of facts and attitudes and introduced, together with technological advances, a multiplicity of moments and ways in which choice intervenes in the process of dying.

However, the medicalization of death which has taken hold in those democratic societies that have recognized the freedom to choose one's death risks forsaking the process of dying as a rich place fraught with subjective meanings. We have seen how the combination of the liberal picture with the medicalization of life has the potentiality to make women's subjectivities in reproduction fade away. Analogously, the liberal picture that defends freedom, and leaves to medicine the understanding and the handling of the wider framework, risks making dying a place inhospitable to subjectivity. In these scenarios, freedom is only anchored to specific moments, to consenting to or refusing of treatment, to the decision of voluntary death, and may be unable to pervade the whole biographical trajectory. Dying is a process run by medical technology and choice is only locally expressed against the background of a scene in which no exercise of, or experimentation with, our subjectivity is called for. There is no chance that in this new context we find the recurrence of images of the good death—the cardiac one—which avoids doctors and machines and increases the desire to die far from hospitals, at home, where we can be ourselves. I have discussed this theme with reference to cancer (Chapter 3, §3.3).

Furthermore, choice itself at the specific moments in which it is made tends to be emptied because the context that can make it meaningful and expressive of one's subjectivity is removed from it. Once the liberal context of choice has been secured we need to assure that the appeal to the autonomy of the patient corresponds with the exercise of her subjectivity. For example, if we are abruptly brought into a hospitalized context, far from our homes, our things, far from those relationships that help us weave the texture of our subjectivity, the very practice of asking for consent might be unable to breach our subjectivities and remains foreign to it. Hilde Lindemann tells the story of an old professor who is woken from sedation to ask if he still wanted the use of artificial ventilation.[10] We can well doubt that in the conditions he is in, which are completely unnatural to him, far from home, from his cat and his music, he is able to express a wish that tells something about himself. Lindemann insists that in cases such as this, subjectivity is expressed in the possibility of leaving others to reveal one's self: in her story, it is perhaps his friend (Lindemann herself) who looks after the personality of the professor most faithfully. Lindemann insists on the relational aspect, but her more general point is that subjectivity is in need of context. In the medicalized conditions of dying, the subject needs to be able to claim the entire process of dying as her own. As with reproduction, in the choices at the end of life, attaining freedoms is of little use if we limit them to selected specific moments of choice and do not see how subjectivity encompasses life in its entirety.

Why should the progress of medicine be secured at the expense of freedom, of the possibility of impressing our unique and personal face to the process of dying? Foucault wrote: "apparently, for the human species life is fragile and death is certain. Why then should we turn this certainty into a chance, to which its sudden and unescapable character bestows on it an aura of punishment?"[11] It surely does not help to make of death something personal belonging to our individual project if we think of it in the mere language of medical explanations and interventions, with its goals and interests that are only partially our goals and interests or sometimes none at all. The scene that is disclosed once freedom and rights have been secured, together with the technology that makes them possible, is that of seizing the process of dying as the expression of our subjectivity, as something that flows from us: that is, as a way in which this radical subjectivity shapes, from its own point of view, the facts and hardness of reality, the fact of disease, of its irreversible character, of our having commenced a path that leads to death. To explore this possibility and mature collectively specific ways of life, together with a reflective awareness of dying that would convey these modalities and novel backgrounds of human life, is a largely new situation that deserves our experimentation.

Notes

1 Saint Thomas Aquinas, *The Summa Theologica*, London: Catholic Way Publishing, 2014, II.II, q. 154, art. 12. For the theoretical framework I rely on Arnold I. Davidson, *The Emergence of Sexuality. Historical Epistemology and the Formation of Concepts*, Cambridge (MA): Harvard University Press, 2001: in particular, "The Horror of Monsters," pp. 93–124.

2 Immanuel Kant, *Lectures on Ethics*, ed. by P. Heath and J.B. Schneewind, Cambridge: Cambridge University Press, 1997, p. 146. See also *The Metaphysics of Morals*, ed. by M. Gregor, Cambridge: Cambridge University Press, 1996, pp. 176 ff.

3 Michel Foucault, *The History of Sexuality. Vol. 2: The Uses of Pleasures*, New York: Vintage Books, 1990, "Introduction."

4 Michel Foucault, *Abnormal*, op. cit. See also David M. Halperin, *One Hundred Years of Homosexuality. And Other Essays on Greek Love*, New York: Routledge, 1990.

5 Michel Foucault, "The Ethics of the Concern for the Self as a Practice of Freedom," op. cit.; "Sex, Power and the Politics of Identity" (1984), in

Foucault Live. Collected Interviews, 1961–1984, ed. by S. Lotringer, New York: Semiotext(e), 1996, pp. 382–390.

6 Michel Foucault, "Interview with Michel Foucault," in *Power. Essential Works of Michel Foucault 1954–1984*, ed. by J. Faubion, New York: The New Press, 2001, pp. 239–297.

7 Immanuel Kant, *Critique of the Power of Judgment*, ed. by P. Guyer, Cambridge: Cambridge University Press, 2000, 1.1.5.

8 In the ways described, for example, by Caterina Botti, *Madri cattive. Una riflessione su bioetica e gravidanza*, Milano: Il Saggiatore, 2007.

9 Carla Lonzi, *Sputiamo su Hegel e altri scritti*, op. cit., p. 40.

10 Hilde Lindemann, "Holding on to Edmund. The Relational Work of Identity," in *Naturalized Bioethics. Toward Responsible Knowing and Practice*, ed. by H. Lindemann, M. Verkerk and M. Urban Walker, Cambridge: Cambridge University Press, 2009, pp. 65–79.

11 Michel Foucault, "Un plaisir si simple," in *Dits et écrits, II, 1976–1988*, Paris: Gallimard, 2001, p. 778.

Index

Taylor & Francis Group
an **informa** business

Taylor & Francis eBooks

www.taylorfrancis.com

A single destination for eBooks from Taylor & Francis with increased functionality and an improved user experience to meet the needs of our customers.

90,000+ eBooks of award-winning academic content in Humanities, Social Science, Science, Technology, Engineering, and Medical written by a global network of editors and authors.

TAYLOR & FRANCIS EBOOKS OFFERS:

A streamlined experience for our library customers

A single point of discovery for all of our eBook content

Improved search and discovery of content at both book and chapter level

REQUEST A FREE TRIAL

support@taylorfrancis.com

Routledge
Taylor & Francis Group

CRC Press
Taylor & Francis Group

For Product Safety Concerns and Information please contact our EU
representative GPSR@taylorandfrancis.com
Taylor & Francis Verlag GmbH, Kaufingerstraße 24, 80331 München, Germany

www.ingramcontent.com/pod-product-compliance
Ingram Content Group UK Ltd.
Pitfield, Milton Keynes, MK11 3LW, UK
UKHW021957180926
475701UK00003B/64
* 9 7 8 1 0 3 2 0 2 0 8 8 4 *